cumbria
marie wallin

contents

foreword

Cumbria is the first of two collections that I designed and photographed last year in 2021. It is a very special collection as it's the first to include menswear! Since I started my design company in 2014, I've had constant requests for men's sweater and cardigan designs. Finally, I've now been able to fulfil these requests with 3 men's designs in Cumbria and 3 in Westmorland, which will be out in early 2023.

The menswear is modelled by James, the handsome 'husband to be' of Georgia, my beautiful model. They are getting married in September this year, I'm so happy for them as they make such a lovely couple, I'm sure you will agree!

The patterned designs in Cumbria are largely inspired by Eastern European folk art and Far East textile and carpet design along with mixtures of more traditional motifs. The plain textured stitch designs are inspired by traditional twisted stitches and cables.

Cumbria is the first collection with the new extended size range. The womens designs are now able to be knitted in 7 sizes - S through to 3XL and the mens designs in 8 sizes - XS through to 3XL. The collection also features six new colours of British Breeds - Acer, Ocean, Seagrass, Storm, Walnut and Willow.

We photographed both Cumbria and Westmorland in the Lake District and Yorkshire Dales National Parks and there are elements of both locations in each of the collections. In the Lakes, we photographed around the village of Elterwater and on the beautiful Langdale Estate. In the Dales, we photographed at the home of my friend Alison O'Neill, at Shacklabank Farm, near Sedbergh. Making his first appearance, is Shadow, Alison's ever faithful dog, hope you spot him! You can read a little more about the locations in the features at the end of the book.

As well as enjoying the new designs, I hope that you also enjoy the beautiful photography in this book! We used a new photographer, Moy Williams. I have worked with Moy many times before whilst I was employed by Rowan and it was a real pleasure to work with him again.

Happy knitting!

bessyboot

is a beautiful Fairisle sweater with a funnel neck and three-quarter length sleeves. The design is a mixture of traditional motifs with other patterning inspired by East European folk art. It has an easy fit silhouette and is knitted flat due to the differing repeating pattern sections. It can be knitted in the round with the introduction of steek stitches where the side seams and armholes would be.

Bessyboot is named after the hill on Rosthwaite Fell in the Lake District National Park.

cumbria

cumbria

bowness

is a very pretty, traditional twisted stitch design. The sweater is fitted, with peplum shaping from the waist and is knitted flat.

Bowness is named after the town on the shores of lake Windermere in South Lakeland, Cumbria.

cumbria

cumbria

troutbeck

is a wonderful, traditionally inspired Fairisle design for men. This easy fit sweater is knitted flat due to the differing repeating pattern sections. It can be knitted in the round with the introduction of steek stitches where the side seams and armholes would be. The Fairisle design itself, is relatively easy to knit as the main colour runs through nearly every pattern section.

Troutbeck is named after the small village in the South Lakes and is situated along the old narrow and hilly coach road from Windermere to Penrith.

cumbria

cumbria

cumbria

catbells

is a pretty Fairisle yoke design which is simple to knit as it is entirely knitted in the round and the main colour runs through nearly all of the patterned sections. It is fitted in shape and can be easily adjusted in length by simply adding more stocking stitch rounds before the start of the pattern.

Catbells is named after a small fell in Barrowdale and is situated on the western shore of Derwentwater in the Lake District National Park.

cumbria

glenridding

is a lovely cardigan for men.
The patterned sections
are inspired by Iranian
and Afghan carpet designs
which are mixed with
more traditional motifs.
The addition of the plaid
border gives the cardigan
a more contemporary
look. It is knitted flat due
to the differing repeating
pattern sections. It can be
knitted in the round with
the introduction of steek
stitches at the centre front
and where the side seams
and armholes would be.

Glenridding is named after
the small tourist village
at the southern end of
Ullswater, near the foot
of the Kirkstone Pass.
The name means 'glen
overgrown with bracken'
and is generally the base for
walkers to climb some of the
highest peaks in the Lake
District.

cumbria

cumbria

keris

is a very sweet
and pretty Fairisle
sleeveless sweater.
The motifs are
inspired by carpet
and ornamental
folk designs of
Eastern Europe
and the Middle
East. It is knitted
flat due to the
differing repeating
pattern sections.
It can be knitted
in the round with
the introduction of
steek stitches where
the side seams and
armholes would be.

Keris is not a
Cumbrian name
but a girl's name
of Welsh origin
meaning 'love'. I
thought it was an
apt name as I like
this design so much!

cumbria

cumbria

lingmoor

is a beautiful and complex Fairisle design inspired by the intricate patterns seen in the carpet designs of Iran, Iraq and Afghanistan. It has a long line fitted silhouette and is knitted flat due to the differing repeating pattern sections. It can be knitted in the round with the introduction of steek stitches where the side seams and armholes would be.

Lingmoor is named after the fell in Ambleside which divides the valleys of Great Langdale and Little Langdale in the Lake District National Park. The name means 'heather covered' and is in my favourite part of the Lakes.

cumbria

cumbria

grasmoor jacket

is a great contemporary cable design for men. It is knitted flat using two ends of the British Breeds yarn together, therefore making it suitable for outdoor wear as a jacket weight cardigan.

Grasmoor is named after the mountain in the northwest of the Lake District. This mountain is characterized by it's very steep western flank which drops dramatically to Crummock Water.

cumbria

rydal

is a very pretty, modern Fairisle design and is relatively simple to knit. This fitted sweater with a slash neck is knitted in the round and has steeked armholes. There is some subtle stitch texture in-between each pattern section adding more interest to the knit.

Rydal is named after a village which lies between Ambleside and Grasmere in Cumbria. It is a significant place in romantic English literature as it was the home of William Wordsworth for many years.

swaledale scarf

is a new version
of the Burra Cowl
from Shetland. This
lovely traditionally
inspired Fairisle Scarf is
completely knitted in
the round. It has small
repeating patterns and
therefore is a great
project for the novice
Fairisle knitter prior to
knitting a whole Fairisle
garment!

Swaledale is named
after the beautiful,
rugged and wild
dale in the north of
the Yorkshire Dales
National Park.

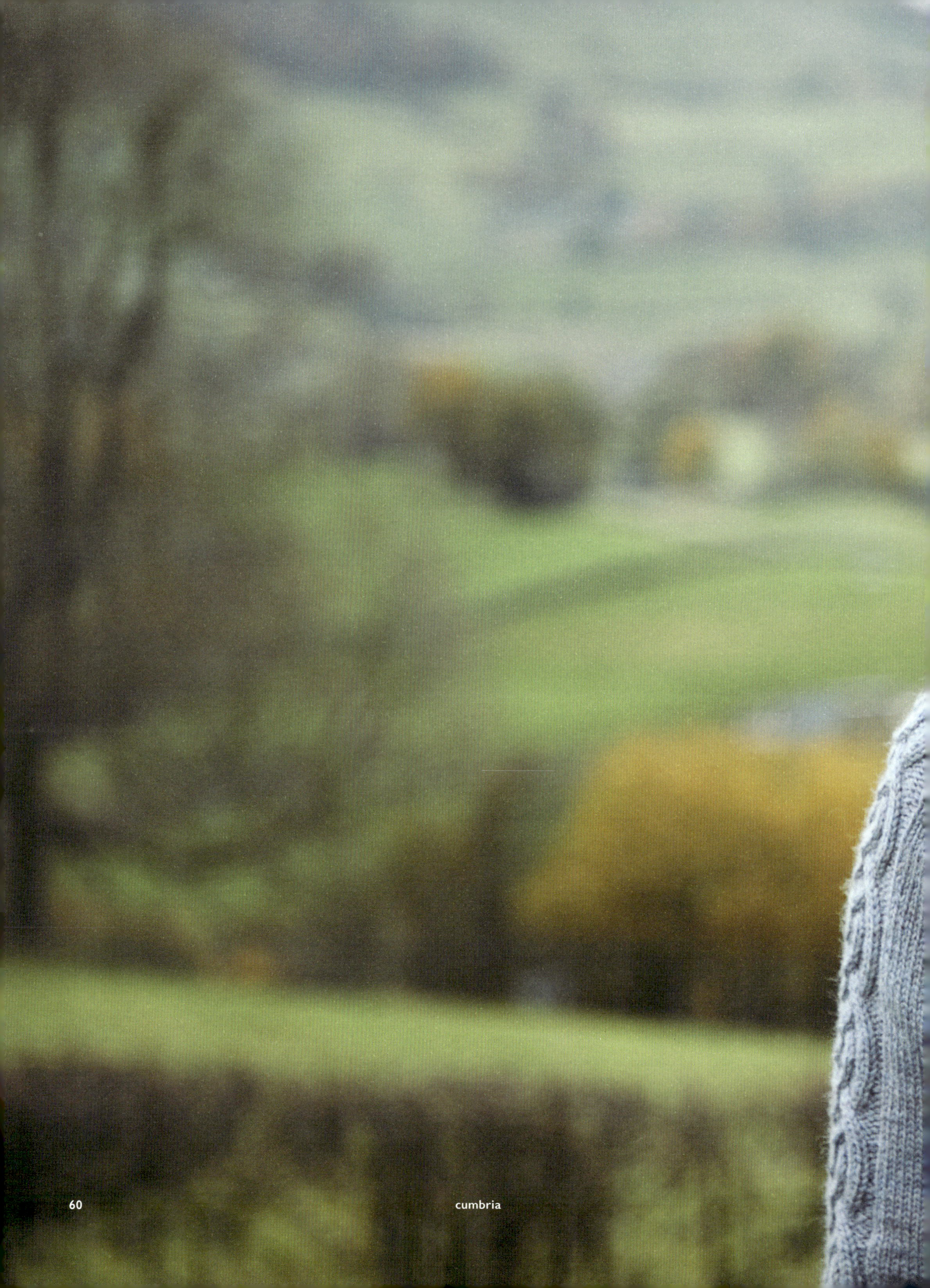

tarn tam

is a lovely
versatile tam
design suitable
for both women
and men. Tams
are the perfect
project for the
novice Fairisle
knitter and
this one is no
exception!

Tarn Tam is
named after
the word tarn,
meaning a small
mountain lake,
generally in a
hollow area
surrounded by
steep slopes.

cumbria

cumbria

65

cumbria

gallery

bessyboot
Main images pages 8 to 13
Pattern page 68

bowness
Main images pages 14 to 19
Pattern page 72

troutbeck
Main images pages 20 to 24
Pattern page 76

catbells
Main images pages 25 to 28
Pattern page 80

grasmoor jacket
Main images pages 47 to 50
Pattern page 84

glenridding
Main images pages 31 to 35
Pattern page 89

keris
Main images pages 36 to 41
Pattern page 94

lingmoor
Main images pages 42 to 46
Pattern page 98

rydal
Main images pages 52 to 57
Pattern page 104

swaledale scarf
Main images pages 58 to 61
Pattern page 110

tarn tam
Main images pages 63 to 65
Pattern page 112

shadow
faithful border collie
and working dog!

bessyboot

Experience ●●●

To fit bust

S	M	L	XL	XXL	2XL	3XL	
81-86	91-97	102-107	112-117	122-127	132-137	142-147	cm
32-34	36-38	40-42	44-46	48-50	52-54	56-58	in

Marie Wallin British Breeds

A Chestnut							
3	3	3	4	4	4	5 × 25gm
B Pale Oak						
4	4	5	5	5	6	6 × 25gm
C Lime Flower						
I	I	2	2	2	2	2 × 25gm
D Dark Apple						
2	2	2	3	3	3	3 × 25gm
E Quince						
2	2	2	2	2	2	2 × 25gm
F Mulberry						
3	3	3	4	4	4	5 × 25gm
G Russet						
2	2	2	2	2	2	2 × 25gm
H Mallard						
2	2	2	2	3	3	3 × 25gm
I Silver Birch						
2	2	2	3	3	3	3 × 25gm
J Rose						
I	I	2	2	2	2	2 × 25gm
K Blossom						
2	2	2	2	2	2	2 × 25gm
L Thistle						
I	I	I	I	2	2	2 × 25gm

Needles
I pair 2³⁄₄mm (no 12) (US 2) needles
I pair 3¹⁄₄mm (no 10) (US 3) needles

Tension
28 sts and 29 rows to 10 cm measured over patterned st st using 3¹⁄₄mm (US 3) needles.

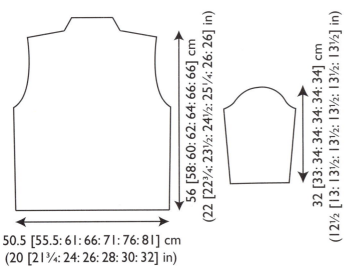

56 [58: 60: 62: 64: 66: 66] cm
(22 [22³⁄₄: 23½: 24½: 25¼: 26: 26] in)

32 [33: 34: 34: 34: 34: 34] cm
(12½ [13: 13½: 13½: 13½: 13½: 13½] in)

50.5 [55.5: 61: 66: 71: 76: 81] cm
(20 [21³⁄₄: 24: 26: 28: 30: 32] in)

BACK and FRONT (both alike)

Using **2¾mm (US 2)** needles and yarn F cast on
141 [155: 171: 185: 199: 213: 227] sts.
Row 1 (RS): K1, *P1, K1, rep from * to end.
Row 2: P1, *K1, P1, rep from * to end.
These 2 rows form rib.
Work in rib for a further 4 rows, ending with **RS** facing for next row.
Change to **3¼mm (US 3)** needles.
Beg and ending rows as indicated, using the **fairisle** technique as described on the information page and repeating the 124 row patt repeat throughout, cont in patt from chart, which is worked entirely in st st beg with a K row, as folls:
Cont straight until work meas 28 [29: 30: 31: 32: 33: 32] cm, ending with **RS** facing for next row.

Shape armholes
Keeping patt correct, cast off 4 sts at beg of next 2 rows.
133 [147: 163: 177: 191: 205: 219] sts.
(**Note:** Armhole shaping is **NOT** shown on chart.)
Dec 1 st at each end of next and foll 4 alt rows.
123 [137: 153: 167: 181: 195: 209] sts.
Cont straight until armhole meas 20 [21: 22: 23: 24: 25: 26] cm, ending with **RS** facing for next row.

Shape shoulders
Cast off 6 [7: 8: 10: 11: 12: 13] sts at beg of next 8 [4: 2: 8: 6: 2: 2] rows, then 7 [8: 9: 11: 12: 13: 14] sts at beg of foll 2 [6: 8: 2: 4: 8: 8] rows.
61 [61: 65: 65: 67: 67: 71] sts.

Shape funnel neck
Dec 1 st at each end of next 5 rows. 51 [51: 55: 55: 57: 57: 61] sts., ending on chart row 40 [46: 52: 58: 64: 70: 70].
Work 1 row, ending with **RS** facing for next row.
Cont in yarn B [F: F: B: B: F: F] **only** as folls:
Change to **2¾mm (US 2)** needles.
Next row (RS): Knit.
Beg with row 2, work in rib as given for cast-on edge for 3 rows, ending with **RS** facing for next row.
Cast off **loosely** in rib.

SLEEVES

Using **2¾mm (US 2)** needles and yarn F cast on
79 [81: 85: 85: 87: 87: 89] sts.
Beg with row 1, work in rib as given for back and front for 6 rows, ending with **RS** facing for next row.
Change to **3¼mm (US 3)** needles.
Beg and ending rows as indicated, cont in patt from chart as folls:
Inc 1 st at each end of 3rd and every foll 8th [6th: 6th: 6th: 6th: 4th: 4th] row to 83 [107: 113: 101: 95: 129: 127] sts, then on every foll 6th [4th: 4th: 4th: 4th: alt: alt] row until there are 107 [113: 117: 123: 129: 135: 141] sts, taking inc sts into patt.
(**Note:** Sleeve shaping is only shown on chart for first 40 rows.)
Work 3 rows, ending after chart row 86 [90: 92: 92: 92: 92: 92] and with **RS** facing for next row.
(Sleeve should meas approx 32 [33: 34: 34: 34: 34: 34] cm.)

Shape top
Keeping patt correct, cast off 4 sts at beg of next 2 rows.
99 [105: 109: 115: 121: 127: 133] sts.
Dec 1 st at each end of next and foll 3 alt rows, then on foll row, ending with **RS** facing for next row.
89 [95: 99: 105: 111: 117: 123] sts.
Cast off.

MAKING UP

Press as described on the information page.
Join both shoulder and funnel neck seams using mattress stitch.
See information page for finishing instructions, setting in sleeves using the shallow set-in method.

■ A. Chestnut   ○ C. Lime Flower   ⏐ E. Quince   ✕ G. Russet   • I. Silver Birch   ◁ K. Blossom

☐ B. Pale Oak   ● D. Dark Apple   ◆ F. Mulberry   ▲ H. Mallard   ▼ J. Rose   ⋀ L. Thistle

Tip!
This chart has been split over two pages. Using the PDF (see info page), print out both halves and join them together

3XL   2XL   XXL   XL   L   M   S

3XL L S
XL M
XXL
2XL

124 row patt rep

S L 3XL
   XL
M XXL
   2XL

cumbria

S   M   L   XL   XXL   2XL   3XL

71

bowness

Experience ●●●

To fit bust

	S	M	L	XL	XXL	2XL	3XL	
	81-86	91-97	102-107	112-117	122-127	132-137	142-147	cm
	32-34	36-38	40-42	44-46	48-50	52-54	56-58	in

Marie Wallin British Breeds

photographed in Raw

18	20	22	24	26	28	30 × 25gm

Needles

1 pair **2¾mm (no 12) (US 2)** knitting needles
1 pair **3¼mm (no 10) (US 3)** knitting needles
Cable needle

Tension

Based on a rev st st tension of 25 sts and 32 rows to 10 cm using
3¼mm (US 3) knitting needles **but** over combination of rev st st and
patts, there will be 40 rows to 10 cm.

32.5 sts and 40 rows to 10 cm measured over sleeve patt using
3¼mm (US 3) knitting needles.

Chart A (32 sts) meas 9 cm wide, chart B (6 sts) meas 2.3 cm wide,
and chart C (22 sts) meas 5.5 cm wide.

SPECIAL ABBREVIATIONS

Cr2L
slip next st onto cable needle and leave at front of work, P1, then K1
from cable needle.

Cr2R
slip next st onto cable needle and leave at back of work, K1, then P1
from cable needle.

Tw2L
K into back of second st on left needle, K tog tbl first 2 sts on left
needle and slip both sts off left needle together.

Tw2R
K2tog leaving sts on left needle, K first st again and slip both sts off
left needle together.

58 [60: 62: 64: 66: 68: 68] cm
(22¾ [23½: 24½: 25¼: 26: 26¾: 26¾] in)

44 [45: 46: 46: 46: 46: 46] cm
(17¼ [17¾: 18: 18: 18: 18: 18] in)

46.5 [51: 56.5: 62.5: 67: 72: 76.5] cm
(18¼ [20: 22¼: 24¼: 26½: 28¼: 30] in)
Chest width is measured
from 2.5cm before the armhole.

BACK

Using **2¾mm (US 2)** needles cast on
224 [236: 250: 264: 276: 288: 300] sts.
Work in g st for 5 rows, ending with **WS** facing for next row.
Change to **3¼mm (US 3)** needles.
Noting that chart row 1 is a **WS** row, now place charts as folls:
Row 1 (WS): K13 [19: 26: 33: 39: 45: 51], work next 22 sts as row 1 of chart C, (work next 30 sts as row 1 of chart B, work next 32 sts as row 1 of chart A) twice, work next 30 sts as row 1 of chart B, work next 22 sts as row 1 of chart C,
K13 [19: 26: 33: 39: 45: 51].
Row 2: P13 [19: 26: 33: 39: 45: 51], work next 22 sts as row 2 of chart C, (work next 30 sts as row 2 of chart B, work next 32 sts as row 2 of chart A) twice, work next 30 sts as row 2 of chart B, work next 22 sts as row 2 of chart C, P13 [19: 26: 33: 39: 45: 51].
These 2 rows set the sts – 7 sets of sts in patt from charts, with edge sts in rev st st.
Keeping sts correct as now set, working appropriate rows and shaping as shown on chart B, repeating the 24 row patt repeat of chart A, and the 20 row patt repeat of chart C, cont until 50 rows have been completed, ending with **WS** facing for next row.
152 [164: 178: 192: 204: 216: 228] sts.
Now repeating **chart rows 53 to 72 only throughout for chart B**, and keeping all other charts correct as set, cont as folls:
Cont straight until back meas 37 [38: 39: 40: 41: 42: 41] cm, ending with **RS** facing for next row.

Shape armholes
Keeping patt correct, cast off 4 [5: 6: 7: 8: 9: 10] sts at beg of next 2 rows. 144 [154: 166: 178: 188: 198: 208] sts.
Dec 1 st at each end of next 5 [5: 7: 7: 9: 9: 9] rows, then on foll 3 [5: 6: 8: 7: 7: 7] alt rows, then on foll 4th row.
126 [132: 138: 146: 154: 164: 174] sts.
Cont straight until armhole meas 18 [19: 20: 21: 22: 23: 24] cm, ending with **RS** facing for next row.

Shape shoulders and back neck
Cast off 4 [5: 5: 5: 6: 6: 7] sts at beg of next 2 rows, then 4 [5: 5: 6: 6: 7: 7] sts at beg of foll 2 rows.
110 [112: 118: 124: 130: 138: 146] sts.
Next row (RS): Cast off 5 [5: 5: 6: 6: 7: 7] sts, patt until there are 26 [27: 28: 30: 31: 34: 36] sts on right needle and turn, leaving rem sts on a holder.
Work each side of neck separately.

Dec 1 st at neck edge of next 6 rows **and at same time** cast off 5 [5: 5: 6: 6: 7: 7] sts at beg of 2nd and foll alt row, then 5 [5: 6: 6: 6: 7: 8] sts at beg of foll alt row.
Work 1 row.
Cast off rem 5 [6: 6: 6: 7: 7: 8] sts.
With **RS** facing, slip centre 48 [48: 52: 52: 56: 56: 60] sts onto a holder (for neckband), rejoin yarn and patt to end.
Complete to match first side, reversing shapings.

FRONT

Work as given for back until 16 [16: 20: 20: 24: 28: 28] rows less have been worked than on back to beg of shoulder shaping, ending with **RS** facing for next row.

Shape front neck
Next row (RS): Patt 48 [51: 54: 58: 62: 69: 72] sts and turn, leaving rem sts on a holder.
Work each side of neck separately.
Keeping patt correct, dec 1 st at neck edge of next 10 rows, then on foll 2 [2: 4: 4: 6: 8: 8] alt rows. 36 [39: 40: 44: 46: 51: 54] sts.
Work 1 row, ending with **RS** facing for next row.

Shape shoulder
Cast off 4 [5: 5: 5: 6: 6: 7] sts at beg of next and foll 1 [5: 4: 0: 5: 0: 4] alt rows, then 5 [-: 6: 6: -: 7: 8] sts at beg of foll 4 [-: 1: 5: -: 5: 1] alt rows **and at same time** dec 1 st at neck edge of next and foll alt row, then on foll 4th row.
Work 1 row.
Cast off rem 5 [6: 6: 6: 7: 7: 8] sts.
With **RS** facing, slip centre 30 [30: 30: 30: 30: 26: 30] sts onto a holder (for neckband), rejoin yarn and patt to end.
Complete to match first side, reversing shapings.

SLEEVES

Using **2¾mm (US 2)** needles cast on 72 [74: 78: 78: 80: 80: 84] sts.
Work in g st for 5 rows, ending with **WS** facing for next row.
Change to **3¼mm (US 3)** needles.
Beg and ending rows as indicated, noting that chart row 1 is a **WS** row and repeating the 20 row patt repeat throughout, cont in patt from sleeve chart as folls:
Inc 1 st at each end of 4th [4th: 4th: 4th: 4th: 2nd: 2nd] and every foll 6th [6th: 6th: 6th: 6th: 4th: 4th] row to 96 [102: 102: 118: 128: 88: 92] sts, then on every foll 8th [8th: 8th: 8th: 8th: 6th: 6th] row until there are

CHART A

CHART B

CHART C

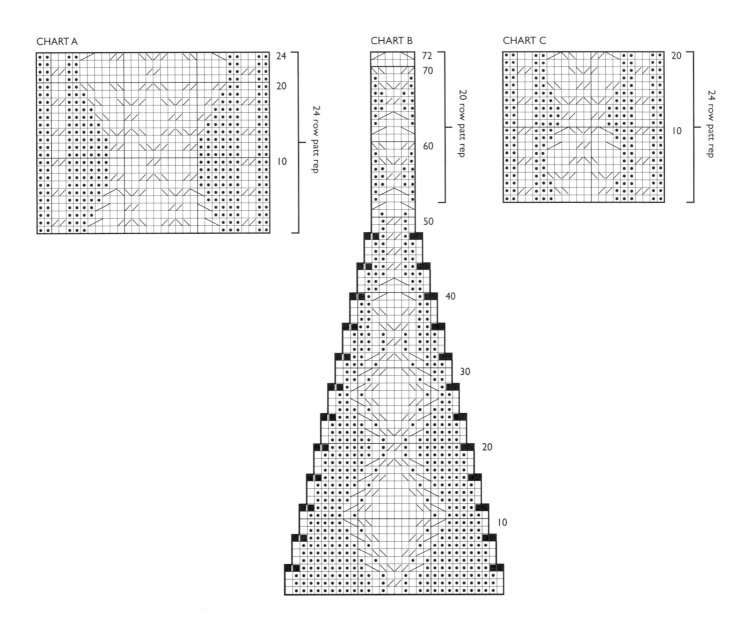

116 [120: 124: 128: 132: 136: 140] sts, taking inc sts into patt.
Cont straight until sleeve meas 44 [45: 46: 46: 46: 46: 46] cm, ending with **RS** facing for next row.

Shape top
Keeping patt correct, cast off 4 [5: 6: 7: 8: 9: 10] sts at beg of

next 2 rows. 108 [110: 112: 114: 116: 118: 120] sts.
Dec 1 st at each end of next 7 rows, then on every foll alt row until 72 sts rem, then on foll 13 rows, ending with **RS** facing for next row. 46 sts.
Cast off 5 sts at beg of next 2 rows, then 6 sts at beg of foll 2 rows.
Cast off rem 24 sts.

cumbria

SLEEVE CHART

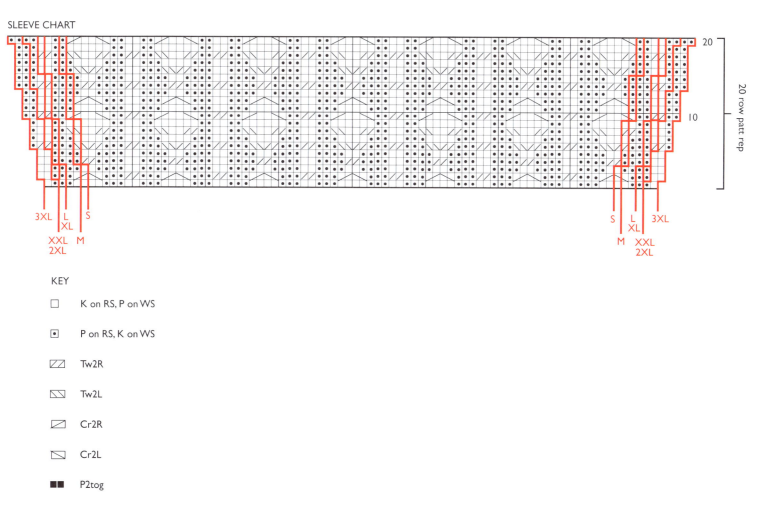

3XL L S
XL
XXL M
2XL

S L 3XL
XL
M XXL
2XL

20

10

20 row patt rep

KEY

☐   K on RS, P on WS

⊡   P on RS, K on WS

⟋   Tw2R

⟍   Tw2L

⟋   Cr2R

⟍   Cr2L

■■   P2tog

MAKING UP

Press as described on the information page.
Join right shoulder seam using mattress stitch.
Neckband
With **RS** facing and using **2¾mm (US 2)** needles, pick up and knit
23 [23: 26: 26: 29: 32: 32] sts down left side of front neck, K across
30 [30: 30: 30: 30: 26: 30] sts on front holder, pick up and knit
23 [23: 26: 26: 29: 32: 32] sts up right side of front neck, and 7 sts
down right side of back neck, K across 48 [48: 52: 52: 56: 56: 60] sts

on back holder dec 3 sts evenly, then pick up and knit 7 sts up left
side of back neck.
135 [135: 145: 145: 155: 157: 165] sts.
Row 1 (WS): P1, *K1, P1, rep from * to end.
Row 2: K1, *P1, K1, rep from * to end.
These 2 rows form rib.
Work in rib for 1 row more, ending with **RS** facing for next row.
Cast off in rib.
See information page for finishing instructions, setting in sleeves using
the set-in method.

troutbeck

Experience ●●○

To fit chest

	XS	S	M	L	XL	XXL	2XL	3XL	
	97-102	102-107	107-112	112-117	117-122	122-127	127-132	132-137	cm
	38-40	40-42	42-44	44-46	46-48	48-50	50-52	52-54	in

Marie Wallin British Breeds

	XS	S	M	L	XL	XXL	2XL	3XL	
A Raw	9	10	10	11	11	12	13	13	× 25gm
B Seagrass	1	2	2	2	2	2	2	2	× 25gm
C Chestnut	2	2	2	2	2	2	2	2	× 25gm
D Eau de Nil	1	1	1	1	1	1	1	1	× 25gm
E Wood	1	1	1	1	1	1	1	1	× 25gm
F Mulberry	1	1	1	1	1	1	1	1	× 25gm
G Walnut	1	1	1	1	1	1	1	2	× 25gm
H Quince	1	1	1	1	1	2	2	2	× 25gm
I Evergreen	1	1	1	1	1	1	1	1	× 25gm
J Thistle	1	1	1	1	1	2	2	2	× 25gm
K Dahlia	1	1	1	1	1	1	1	1	× 25gm
L Ocean	1	1	1	2	2	2	2	2	× 25gm
M Silver Birch	1	2	2	2	2	2	2	2	× 25gm
N Mallard	2	2	2	2	2	2	2	3	× 25gm
O Willow	1	1	1	1	1	1	1	1	× 25gm
P Lime Flower	1	1	1	1	1	1	1	1	× 25gm
Q Russet	1	1	1	1	1	1	1	1	× 25gm

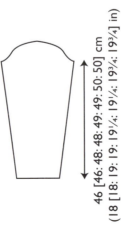

64 [66: 68: 70: 70: 72: 72: 72] cm
(25¼ [26: 26¾: 27½: 27½: 28¼: 28¼: 28¼] in)

50.5 [53: 55.5: 58: 60.5: 63: 66: 68] cm
(20 [20¾: 21¾: 22¾: 23¾: 24¾: 26: 26¾] in)

46 [46: 48: 48: 49: 49: 50: 50] cm
(18 [18: 19: 19: 19¼: 19¼: 19¾: 19¾] in)

Needles
I pair 2¾mm (no 12) (US 2) needles
I pair 3¼mm (no 10) (US 3) needles
2¾mm (no 12) (US 2) circular needle

Tension
28 sts and 29 rows to 10 cm measured over patterned st st using
3¼mm (US 3) needles.

Chart note: Chart pattern repeat is an **odd** number of rows. On first
rep of chart, work odd numbered rows as **RS knit** rows, reading chart
from right to left. On second rep of chart, work odd numbered rows
as **WS purl** rows, reading chart from left to right.

BACK
Using 2¾mm (US 2) needles and yarn N cast on
141 [149: 155: 163: 169: 177: 185: 191] sts.
Break off yarn N and join in yarn A.
Row 1 (RS): KI, *PI, KI, rep from * to end.
Row 2: PI, *KI, PI, rep from * to end.
These 2 rows form rib.
Cont in rib until work meas 7 cm, ending with **RS** facing for next row.
Change to 3¼mm (US 3) needles.
Beg and ending rows as indicated, using the **fairisle** technique as
described on the information page and repeating the 99 row patt
repeat as required (see chart note), cont in patt from chart, which is
worked entirely in st st beg with a K row, as folls:
Cont straight until back meas 38 [40: 40: 41: 40: 41: 40: 40] cm,
ending with **RS** facing for next row.

Shape armholes
Keeping patt correct, cast off 6 sts at beg of next 2 rows.
129 [137: 143: 151: 157: 165: 173: 179] sts.
(**Note:** Armhole shaping is **NOT** shown on chart.)
Dec I st at each end of next and foll 7 alt rows.
113 [121: 127: 135: 141: 149: 157: 163] sts.
Cont straight until armhole meas 23 [23: 25: 26: 27: 28: 29: 29] cm,
ending with **RS** facing for next row.

Shape shoulders and back neck
Cast off 6 [7: 7: 8: 8: 9: 10: 10] sts at beg of next 2 rows.
101 [107: 113: 119: 125: 131: 137: 143] sts.
Next row (RS): Cast off 6 [7: 7: 8: 9: 9: 10: 10] sts, patt until there are
25 [27: 28: 30: 31: 32: 34: 37] sts on right needle and turn, leaving
rem sts on a holder.
Work each side of neck separately.
Keeping patt correct, dec I st at neck edge of next 4 rows **and at**

same time cast off 7 [7: 8: 8: 9: 9: 10: 11] sts at beg of 2nd row,
then 7 [8: 8: 9: 9: 9: 10: 11] sts at beg of foll alt row.
Work I row.
Cast off rem 7 [8: 8: 9: 9: 10: 10: 11] sts.
With **RS** facing, slip centre 39 [39: 43: 43: 45: 49: 49: 49] sts onto a
holder (for neckband), rejoin appropriate yarns and patt to end.
Complete to match first side, reversing shapings.

FRONT
Work as given for back until 30 [30: 30: 32: 32: 36: 36: 36] rows less
have been worked than on back to beg of shoulder shaping, ending
with **RS** facing for next row.
Divide for front neck
Next row (RS): Patt 56 [60: 63: 67: 70: 74: 78: 81] sts and turn, leaving
rem sts on a holder.
Work each side of neck separately.
Keeping patt correct, dec I st at neck edge of next
12 [12: 16: 14: 16: 16: 16: 16] rows, then on foll
8 [8: 6: 8: 7: 9: 9: 9] alt rows.
36 [40: 41: 45: 47: 49: 53: 56] sts.
Work I row, ending with **RS** facing for next row.

Shape shoulder
Cast off 6 [7: 7: 8: 8: 9: 10: 10] sts at beg of next and foll
1 [2: 1: 2: 0: 3: 3: 1] alt rows, then 7 [8: 8: 9: 9: -: -: 11] sts at beg of foll
2 [1: 2: 1: 3: -: -: 2] alt rows **and at same time** dec I st at neck edge of
next and foll 2 alt rows.
Work I row.
Cast off rem 7 [8: 8: 9: 9: 10: 10: 11] sts.
With **RS** facing, slip centre st onto a holder (for neckband), rejoin
appropriate yarns and patt to end.
56 [60: 63: 67: 70: 74: 78: 81] sts.
Complete to match first side, reversing shapings.

SLEEVES
Using 2¾mm (US 2) needles and yarn N cast on
61 [61: 65: 65: 67: 71: 73: 73] sts.
Break off yarn N and join in yarn A.
Beg with row I, work in rib as given for back for 7 cm, ending with **RS**
facing for next row.
Change to 3¼mm (US 3) needles.
Beg and ending rows as indicated, cont in patt from chart as folls:
Inc I st at each end of 3rd and every foll alt row to
87 [87: 101: 113: 115: 123: 131: 131] sts, then on every foll 4th row until
there are 123 [123: 135: 141: 145: 151: 157: 157] sts, taking inc sts into
patt. (**Note:** Sleeve shaping is only shown on chart for first 40 rows.)

KEY

- □ A. Raw
- × B. Seagrass
- ■ C. Chestnut
- △ D. Eau de Nil
- ● E. Wood
- ⬬ F. Mulberry
- ★ G. Walnut
- • H. Quince
- + I. Evergreen
- ▲ J. Thistle
- ▼ K. Dahlia
- ◆ L. Ocean
- ○ M. Silver Birch
- ⬮ N. Mallard
- ◢ O. Willow
- – P. Lime Flower
- ∪ Q. Russet

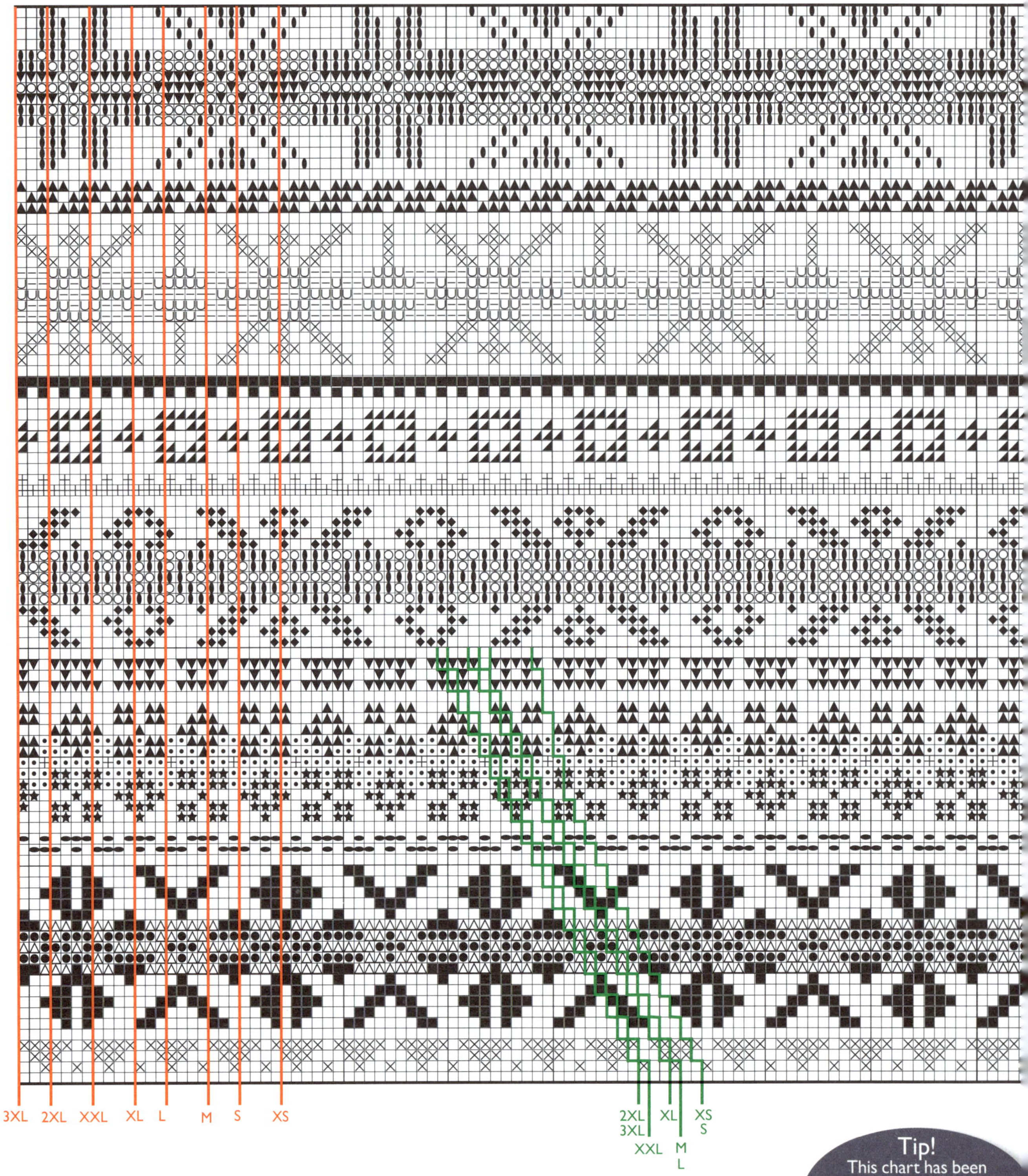
3XL
2XL
XXL
XL
L
M
S
XS
2XL
3XL
XXL
XL
M
L
XS
S

Tip!
This chart has been split over two pages. Using the PDF (see info page), print out both halves and join them together

Cont straight until sleeve meas 46 [46: 48: 48: 49: 49: 50: 50] cm, ending with **RS** facing for next row.

Shape top

Keeping patt correct, cast off 6 sts at beg of next 2 rows.
111 [111: 123: 129: 133: 139: 145: 145] sts.
Dec 1 st at each end of next and foll 6 alt rows, then on foll row, ending with **RS** facing fo next row.
Cast off rem 95 [95: 107: 113: 117: 123: 129: 129] sts.

MAKING UP

Press as described on the information page.
Join both shoulder seams using mattress stitch.

Neckband

With **RS** facing, using **2¾mm (US 2)** circular needle and yarn A, pick up and knit 38 [38: 38: 40: 40: 44: 44: 44] sts down left side of front neck, K st on holder at base of V and mark this st with a coloured thread, pick up and knit 38 [38: 38: 40: 40: 44: 44: 44] sts up right

side of front neck, and 5 sts down right side of back neck, K across
39 [39: 43: 43: 45: 49: 49: 49] sts on back holder, then pick up and
knit 5 sts up left side of back neck.

126 [126: 130: 134: 136: 148: 148: 148] sts.

Round 1 (RS): *K1, P1, rep from * to end.

This round forms the rib.

Keeping rib correct, cont as folls:

Round 2: Rib to within 1 st of marked st, slip next 2 sts as though

to K2tog (marked st is 2nd of these 2 sts), K1, then pass 2 slipped sts
over, rib to end.

Rep last round 3 times more.

118 [118: 122: 126: 128: 140: 140: 140] sts.

Break off yarn A and join in yarn N.

Cast off in rib, still decreasing either side of marked st as before.

See information page for finishing instructions, setting in sleeves using
shallow set-in method.

catbells

Experience ●●○

To fit bust

	S	M	L	XL	XXL	2XL	3XL	
	81-86	91-97	102-107	112-117	122-127	132-137	142-147	cm
	32-34	36-38	40-42	44-46	48-50	52-54	56-58	in

Marie Wallin British Breeds

A Raw								
	10	12	13	14	16	17	18 × 25gm	
B Rose								
	1	1	2	2	2	2	2 × 25gm	
C Quince								
	1	1	1	1	1	1	1 × 25gm	
D Russet								
	1	1	1	1	1	1	1 × 25gm	
E Wood								
	1	1	1	1	1	1	1 × 25gm	
F Foxglove								
	1	1	1	1	1	1	1 × 25gm	
G Mallard								
	1	1	1	1	2	2	2 × 25gm	
H Walnut								
	1	1	1	1	1	1	1 × 25gm	
I Silver Birch								
	1	1	1	1	1	1	1 × 25gm	
J Dark Apple								
	1	1	1	1	1	1	1 × 25gm	
K Thistle								
	1	1	1	1	1	1	1 × 25gm	
L Blossom								
	1	1	1	1	1	1	1 × 25gm	

Needles
2¼mm (no 13) (US 1) circular needle
2¾mm (no 12) (US 2) circular needle
3¼mm (no 10) (US 3) circular needle
Set of 4 double-pointed 2¼mm (no 13) (US 1) needles
Set of 4 double-pointed 2¾mm (no 12) (US 2) needles
Set of 4 double-pointed 3¼mm (no 10) (US 3) needles

Tension
28 sts and 36 rounds to 10 cm measured over plain st st using **2¾mm (US 2)** circular needle. 28 sts and 29 rounds to 10 cm measured over patterned st st using **3¼mm (US 3)** circular needle.

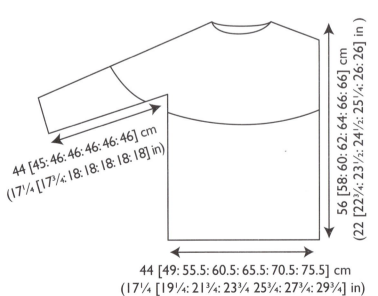

44 [45: 46: 46: 46: 46: 46] cm
(17¼ [17¾: 18: 18: 18: 18: 18] in)

56 [58: 60: 62: 64: 66: 66] cm
(22 [22¾: 23½: 24½: 25¼: 26: 26] in)

44 [49: 55.5: 60.5: 65.5: 70.5: 75.5] cm
(17¼ [19¼: 21¾: 23¾ 25¾: 27¾: 29¾] in)

BODY (worked in one piece to armholes)

Using **2¼mm (US 1)** circular needle and yarn A cast on
246 [274: 310: 338: 366: 394: 422] sts.

Taking care not to twist cast-on edge and placing a marker on first st of next round (to denote right side "seam"), cont as folls:

Round 1 (RS): *K1, P1, rep from * to end.

This round forms the rib.

Cont in rib until work meas 7 cm.

Change to **2¾mm (US 2)** circular needle.

Now work in st st (K every round) until work meas
23 [24: 25.5: 26.5: 27.5: 28.5: 28] cm from cast on edge.

Change to **3¼mm (US 3)** circular needle.

Beg and ending rounds as indicated, using the **fairisle** technique as described on the information page, cont in patt from body chart, which is worked entirely in st st (K every round), positioning chart as folls:

Next round (RS): *Work first 1 [8: 5: 0: 7: 2: 9] sts of chart, work 24 st patt repeat 5 [5: 6: 7: 7: 8: 8] times, work next 2 [9: 6: 1: 8: 3: 10] sts of chart, rep from * once more.

This round sets position of chart.

Cont as now set until all 20 rounds of chart have been completed. Break yarns and join in yarn A.

Next round (RS): K4 and slip these 4 sts onto a safety pin (for right underarm), K next 57 [64: 73: 80: 87: 94: 101] sts and slip these sts onto a holder (for right back), K next 57 [64: 73: 80: 87: 94: 101] sts and slip these sts onto another holder (for left back), K9 and slip these 9 sts onto another safety pin (for left underarm), K next 114 [128: 146: 160: 174: 188: 202] sts and slip these sts onto another holder (for front), K rem 5 sts and slip these 5 sts onto same safety pin as 4 sts at beg of round (9 sts now on this safety pin – for right underarm). Break off yarn.

SLEEVES

Using set of 4 double-pointed **2¼mm (US 1)** needles and yarn A cast on 56 [58: 62: 62: 64: 64: 68] sts.

Distribute sts evenly over 3 of the 4 needles and, taking care not to twist cast-on edge and placing a marker on first st of next round (to denote sleeve "seam"), cont as folls:

Work in rib as given for body for 7 cm, inc 1 st at end of last round. 57 [59: 63: 63: 65: 65: 69] sts.

Move marker onto last st of last round – this is now sleeve "seam" st.

Change to double-pointed **2¾mm (US 2)** needles.

Now work in st st (K every round) as folls:

Work 2 rounds.

Next round (RS): K1, M1, K to last 2 sts, M1, K1, K marked sleeve "seam" st.

Working all sleeve increases as set by last round, inc 1 st at each end of 4th and 10 [11: 9: 15: 18: 24: 24] foll 4th rounds, then on 10 [10: 12: 8: 6: 2: 2] foll 6th rounds.
101 [105: 109: 113: 117: 121: 125] sts.

Work 1 round.

Change to **3¼mm (US 3)** circular needle.

Beg and ending rounds as indicated, using the **fairisle** technique as described on the information page, cont in patt from sleeve chart, which is worked entirely in st st (K every round), positioning chart as folls:

Next round (RS): Work first 2 [4: 6: 8: 10: 12: 14] sts of chart, work 24 st patt repeat 4 times, work last 3 [5: 7: 9: 11: 13: 15] sts of chart.

This round sets position of chart.

Cont straight until all 20 rounds of chart have been completed. Break yarns and join in yarn A.

Next round (RS): K4 and slip these 4 sts onto a safety pin (for underarm), K next 92 [96: 100: 104: 108: 112: 116] sts and slip these sts onto a holder (for sleeve), K rem 5 sts and slip these 5 sts onto same safety pin as 4 sts at beg of round (9 sts now on this safety pin – for underarm).

Break off yarn.

YOKE

Pattern note: As the number of sts decreases, change to double-pointed needles.

With **RS** facing, using **3¼mm (US 3)** circular needle and yarn A, K across sts on holders as folls: K across 57 [64: 73: 80: 87: 94: 101] sts on left back holder, K across 92 [96: 100: 104: 108: 112: 116] sts on left sleeve holder, K across 114 [128: 146: 160: 174: 188: 202] sts on front holder, K across 92 [96: 100: 104: 108: 112: 116] sts on right sleeve holder, and then K across 57 [64: 73: 80: 87: 94: 101] sts on right back holder. 412 [448: 492: 528: 564: 600: 636] sts.

Place marker on first st of last round – this is centre back st.

Next round: K10 [19: 10: 27: 16: 15: 33], K2tog, (K8 [6: 8: 6: 7: 6: 6], K2tog) 39 [51: 47: 59: 59: 71: 71] times, K10 [19: 10: 27: 15: 15: 33]. 372 [396: 444: 468: 504: 528: 564] sts.

Using yarn A, work 0 [1: 1: 2: 3: 4: 5] rounds.

Beg and ending rounds as indicated and using the **fairisle** technique as described on the information page, cont in patt from chart A, which is worked entirely in st st (K every round), as folls:

Repeating the 12 st patt repeat 31 [33: 37: 39: 42: 44: 47] times around each round, work rounds 1 to 13.

Next round: Using yarn J, K10 [9: 10: 27: 15: 15: 33], K2tog, (K8 [6: 7: 5: 6: 5: 5], K2tog) 35 [47: 47: 59: 59: 71: 71] times, K10 [9: 9: 26: 15: 14: 32]. 336 [348: 396: 408: 444: 456: 492] sts.

Now repeating the 12 st patt repeat 28 [29: 33: 34: 37: 38: 41] times around each round, work rounds 15 to 27.

Next round: Using yarn J, K3 [9: 9: 26: 15: 14: 32], K2tog, (K5 [5: 6: 4: 5: 4: 4], K2tog) 47 [47: 47: 59: 59: 71: 71] times, K2 [8: 9: 26: 14: 14: 32]. 288 [300: 348: 348: 384: 384: 420] sts.
Now repeating the 12 st patt repeat 24 [25: 29: 29: 32: 32: 35] times around each round, work rounds 29 to 37.
Using yarn A, work 0 [0: 0: 1: 1: 1: 1] round.
Next round: Using yarn A, K7 [22: 20: 20: 2: 2: 8], K2tog, (K5 [3: 4: 4: 4: 4: 4], K2tog) 39 [51: 51: 51: 63: 63: 67] times, K6 [21: 20: 20: 2: 2: 8]. 248 [248: 296: 296: 320: 320: 352] sts.
Using yarn A, work 0 [0: 1: 1: 2: 3: 4] rounds.
Beg and ending rounds as indicated and using the **fairisle** technique as described on the information page, cont in patt from chart B, which is worked entirely in st st (K every round), as folls:
Repeating the 8 st patt repeat 31 [31: 37: 37: 40: 40: 44] times around each round, work rounds 1 to 10.
Next round: Using yarn A, K6 [6: 10: 10: 2: 2: 33], K2tog, (K3 [3: 3: 3: 3: 3: 2], K2tog) 47 [47: 55: 55: 63: 63: 71] times, K5 [5: 9: 9: 1: 1: 33]. 200 [200: 240: 240: 256: 256: 280] sts.
Now repeating the 8 st patt repeat 25 [25: 30: 30: 32: 32: 35] times around each round, work rounds 12 to 26.
Using yarn A, work 0 [0: 1: 1: 1: 1: 1] round.
Next round: Using yarn A, K13 [13: 1: 1: 1: 1: 1], K2tog, (K2, K2tog) 43 [43: 59: 59: 63: 63: 69] times, K13 [13: 1: 1: 1: 1: 1].
156 [156: 180: 180: 192: 192: 210] sts.
Using yarn A, work 0 [1: 1: 2: 3: 4: 4] rounds.
Beg and ending rounds as indicated and using the **fairisle** technique as described on the information page, cont in patt from chart C, which is worked entirely in st st (K every round), as folls:
Repeating the 6 st patt repeat 26 [26: 30: 30: 32: 32: 35] times around each round, work rounds 1 to 5.
Break off yarn G and cont in yarn A only.
Next round: K18 [18: 8: 8: 6: 6: 0], (K2tog, K1, K2tog) 24 [24: 33: 33: 36: 36: 42] times, K18 [18: 7: 7: 6: 6: 0].
108 [108: 114: 114: 120: 120: 126] sts.
Knit 2 rounds.

Work neckband
Change to double-pointed 2¼mm (US 1) needles.
Now work in rib as given for cast-on edge of body for 5 rounds.
Cast off **loosely** in rib.

MAKING UP
Press as described on the information page.
See information page for finishing instructions, joining both body and sleeve underarm seams by grafting together each set of 9 sts left on safety pins.

CHART A

12 st patt rep

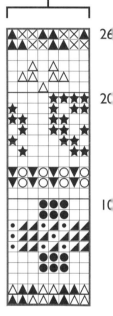

CHART B

8 st patt rep

CHART C

6 st patt rep

KEY

□	A. Raw	◆	G. Mallard
■	B. Rose	▼	H. Walnut
•	C. Quince	○	I. Silver Birch
●	D. Russet	◢	J. Dark Apple
▲	E. Wood	★	K. Thistle
△	F. Foxglove	✕	L. Blossom

BODY CHART

24 st patt rep

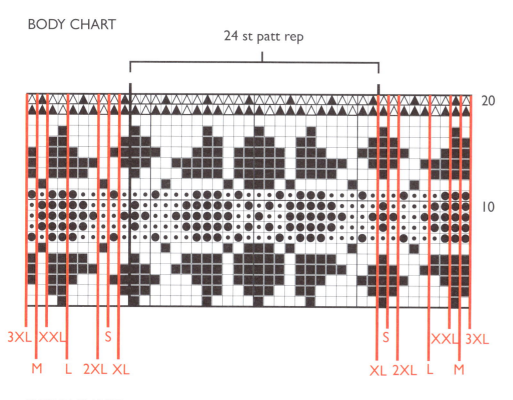

20

10

3XL XXL   S   S   XXL 3XL
   M   L   2XL XL   XL 2XL L   M

SLEEVE CHART

24 st patt rep

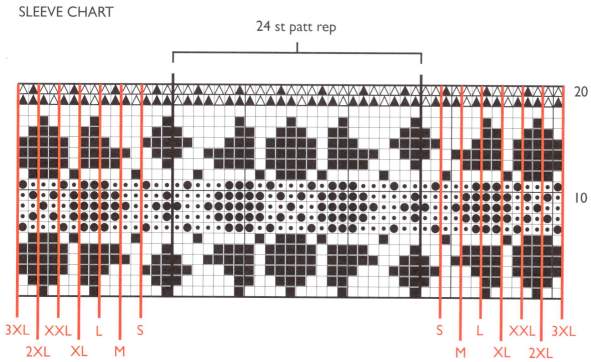

20

10

3XL   XXL   L   S   S   L   XXL   3XL
   2XL   XL   M   M   XL   2XL

grasmoor jacket

Experience ●●●

To fit chest

XS	S	M	L	XL	XXL	2XL	3XL	
97-102	102-107	107-112	112-117	117-122	122-127	127-132	132-137	cm
38-40	40-42	42-44	44-46	46-48	48-50	50-52	52-54	in

Marie Wallin British Breeds

photographed in Storm

| 41 | 44 | 47 | 51 | 53 | 57 | 60 | 61 | × 25gm |

Needles
1 pair **3¾mm (no 9) (US 5)** needles
1 pair **4½mm (no 7) (US 7)** needles
Cable needle

Buttons
9 × TGB 4677 – 23mm from Textile Garden, see information page for contact details.

Tension
Based on a st st tension of 19 sts and 26 rows to 10 cm using **4½mm (US 7)** needles and yarn DOUBLE.
Moss st tension is 20 sts to 10 cm and row tension is 30 rows to 10 cm over patts using **4½mm (US 7)** needles and yarn DOUBLE.
Diamond cable – panel A and panel E (16 sts) each measure 5.2 cm.
Moss st cable – panel B and panel D (8 sts) each measure 3.3 cm.
Cable hearts panel – panel C (55 sts) measures 20 cm.

SPECIAL ABBREVIATIONS

C6B = slip next 3 sts onto cable needle and leave at back of work, K3, then K3 from cable needle;

C6F = slip next 3 sts onto cable needle and leave at front of work, K3, then K3 from cable needle;

C8B = slip next 4 sts onto cable needle and leave at back of work, K4, then K4 from cable needle;

C8F = slip next 4 sts onto cable needle and leave at front of work, K4, then K4 from cable needle;

Cr2L = slip next st onto cable needle and leave at front of work, P1, then K1 from cable needle;

Cr2R = slip next st onto cable needle and leave at back of work, K1, then P1 from cable needle;

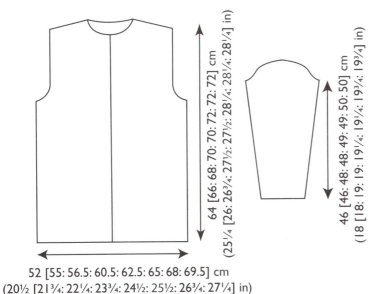

64 [66: 68: 70: 70: 72: 72: 72] cm
(25¼ [26: 26¾: 27½: 27½: 28¼: 28¼: 28¼] in)

46 [46: 48: 48: 49: 49: 50: 50] cm
(18 [18: 19: 19: 19¼: 19¼: 19¾: 19¾] in)

52 [55: 56.5: 60.5: 62.5: 65: 68: 69.5] cm
(20½ [21¾: 22¼: 23¾: 24½: 25½: 26¾: 27¼] in)

Cr4L = slip next 3 sts onto cable needle and leave at front of work, P1, then K3 from cable needle;

Cr4R = slip next 1 st onto cable needle and leave at back of work, K3, then P1 from cable needle;

Cr5L = slip next 3 sts onto cable needle and leave at front of work, P2, then K3 from cable needle;

Cr5R = slip next 2 sts onto cable needle and leave at back of work, K3, then P2 from cable needle.

PANEL/CHART NOTE: All even rows on all the charts are worked as RS rows.

When working panels B and D, work chart row 1 once only, then repeat chart rows 2 to 21 throughout as a 20 row patt repeat.

BACK

Using **3¾mm (US 5)** needles and yarn DOUBLE cast on 146 [154: 158: 166: 170: 178: 182: 186] sts.

Row 1 (RS): K2, *P2, K2, rep from * to end.

Row 2: P2, *K2, P2, rep from * to end.

These 2 rows form rib.

Work in rib for a further 13 rows, inc 1 [0: 0: 1: 1: 0: 1: 1] st at each end of last row and ending with **WS** facing for next row.
148 [154: 158: 168: 172: 178: 184: 188] sts.

Change to **4½mm (US 7)** needles.

Now work in patt, placing patt panels as folls:

Row 1 (WS): K1 [0: 0: 1: 1: 0: 1: 1], (P1, K1) 1 [3: 4: 2: 3: 5: 6: 7] times, work next 16 sts as row 1 of panel E, (work next 8 sts as row 1 of panel D – see panel/chart note) 0 [0: 0: 1: 1: 1: 1: 1] times, work next 55 sts as row 1 of panel C, work next 55 sts as row 35 of panel C, (work next 8 sts as row 1 of panel B – see panel/chart note) 0 [0: 0: 1: 1: 1: 1: 1] times, work next 16 sts as row 1 of panel A, (K1, P1) 1 [3: 4: 2: 3: 5: 6: 7] times, K1 [0: 0: 1: 1: 0: 1: 1].

Row 2 (RS): K1 [0: 0: 1: 1: 0: 1: 1], (P1, K1) 1 [3: 4: 2: 3: 5: 6: 7] times, work next 16 sts as row 2 of panel A, (work next 8 sts as row 2 of panel B) 0 [0: 0: 1: 1: 1: 1: 1] times, work next 55 sts as row 36 of panel C, work next 55 sts as row 2 of panel C, (work next 8 sts as row 2 of panel D) 0 [0: 0: 1: 1: 1: 1: 1] times, work next 16 sts as row 2 of panel E, (K1, P1) 1 [3: 4: 2: 3: 5: 6: 7] times, K1 [0: 0: 1: 1: 0: 1: 1].

These 2 rows set the sts – patt panels with 3 [6: 8: 5: 7: 10: 13: 15] sts at side seams in moss st.

Working appropriate rows of panels, repeating the 26 row (for panels A and E), 20 row (for panels B and D) and 68 row (for panel C) patt repeats throughout and keeping sts correct as now set, cont as folls:
Cont straight until back meas 38 [40: 40: 41: 40: 41: 40: 40] cm, ending with **RS** facing for next row.

Shape armholes

Keeping patt correct, cast off 5 sts at beg of next 2 rows.
138 [144: 148: 158: 162: 168: 174: 178] sts.
Dec 1 st at each end of next and foll 6 alt rows.
124 [130: 134: 144: 148: 154: 160: 164] sts.
Cont straight until armhole meas 23 [23: 25: 26: 27: 28: 29: 29] cm, ending with **RS** facing for next row.

Shape shoulders and back neck

Cast off 8 [8: 8: 9: 9: 10: 10: 11] sts at beg of next 2 rows.
108 [114: 118: 126: 130: 134: 140: 142] sts.

Next row (RS): Cast off 8 [8: 8: 9: 10: 10: 10: 11] sts, patt until there are 28 [31: 31: 34: 34: 34: 37: 37] sts on right needle and turn, leaving rem sts on a holder.

Work each side of neck separately.

Keeping patt correct, dec 1 st at neck edge of next 4 rows **and at same time** cast off 8 [9: 9: 10: 10: 10: 11: 11] sts at beg of 2nd and foll alt row.

Work 1 row.

Cast off rem 8 [9: 9: 10: 10: 10: 11: 11] sts.

With **RS** facing, slip centre 36 [36: 40: 40: 42: 46: 46: 46] sts onto a holder (for neckband), rejoin yarn and patt to end.

Complete to match first side, reversing shapings.

LEFT FRONT

Using **3¾mm (US 5)** needles and yarn DOUBLE cast on 75 [75: 79: 83: 83: 87: 91: 91] sts.

Row 1 (RS): K2, *P2, K2, rep from * to last st, K1.

Row 2: K1, P2, *K2, P2, rep from * to end.

These 2 rows form rib.

Work in rib for a further 13 rows, dec [inc: -: inc: inc: inc: inc: inc] 1 [2: 0: 1: 3: 2: 1: 3] sts evenly across last row and ending with **WS** facing for next row. 74 [77: 79: 84: 86: 89: 92: 94] sts.

Change to **4½mm (US 7)** needles.

Now work in patt, placing cable panels as folls:

Row 1 (WS): Work first 55 sts as row 35 of panel C, (work next 8 sts as row 1 of panel B – see panel/chart note) 0 [0: 0: 1: 1: 1: 1: 1] times, work next 16 sts as row 1 of panel A, (K1, P1) 1 [3: 4: 2: 3: 5: 6: 7] times, K1 [0: 0: 1: 1: 0: 1: 1].

Row 2: K1 [0: 0: 1: 1: 0: 1: 1], (P1, K1) 1 [3: 4: 2: 3: 5: 6: 7] times, work next 16 sts as row 2 of panel A, (work next 8 sts as row 2 of panel B) 0 [0: 0: 1: 1: 1: 1: 1] times, work next 55 sts as row 36 of panel C.

These 2 rows set the sts – patt panels with 3 [6: 8: 5: 7: 10: 13: 15] sts at side seam in moss st.

Working appropriate rows of panels and keeping sts correct as now set, cont as folls:

Cont straight until left front matches back to beg of armhole shaping, ending with **RS** facing for next row.

Shape armhole

Keeping patt correct, cast off 5 sts at beg of next row.
69 [72: 74: 79: 81: 84: 87: 89] sts.
Work 1 row.
Dec 1 st at armhole edge of next and foll 6 alt rows.
62 [65: 67: 72: 74: 77: 80: 82] sts.
Cont straight until 8 [8: 8: 10: 10: 12: 12: 12] rows less have been worked than on back to beg of shoulder shaping, ending with **RS** facing for next row.

Shape front neck

Next row (RS): Patt 50 [53: 53: 59: 60: 62: 65: 67] sts and turn, leaving rem 12 [12: 14: 13: 14: 15: 15: 15] sts on a holder (for neckband).
Keeping patt correct, dec 1 st at neck edge of next
7 [7: 7: 8: 8: 8: 8: 8] rows, then on foll 0 [0: 0: 0: 0: 1: 1: 1] alt row.
43 [46: 46: 51: 52: 53: 56: 58] sts.
Work 0 [0: 0: 1: 1: 1: 1: 1] row, ending with **RS** facing for next row.

Shape shoulder

Keeping patt correct, cast off 8 [8: 8: 9: 9: 10: 10: 11] sts at beg of next and foll 3 [1: 1: 1: 0: 3: 1: 3] alt rows, then – [9: 9: 10: 10: -: 11: -] sts at beg of foll – [2: 2: 2: 3: -: 2: -] alt rows **and at same time** dec 1 st at neck edge of next and foll 2 alt rows.
Work 1 row.
Cast off rem 8 [9: 9: 10: 10: 10: 11: 11] sts.

RIGHT FRONT

Using **3¾mm (US 5)** needles and yarn DOUBLE cast on
75 [75: 79: 83: 83: 87: 91: 91] sts.
Row 1 (RS): K3, *P2, K2, rep from * to end.
Row 2: P2, *K2, P2, rep from * to last st, K1.
These 2 rows form rib.
Work in rib for a further 13 rows, dec [inc: -: inc: inc: inc: inc: inc]
1 [2: 0: 1: 3: 2: 1: 3] sts evenly across last row and ending with **WS** facing for next row. 74 [77: 79: 84: 86: 89: 92: 94] sts.
Change to **4½mm (US 7)** needles.
Now work in patt, placing cable panels as folls:
Row 1 (WS): K1 [0: 0: 1: 1: 0: 1: 1], (P1, K1) 1 [3: 4: 2: 3: 5: 6: 7] times, work next 16 sts as row 1 of panel E, (work next 8 sts as row 1 of panel D – see panel/chart note) 0 [0: 0: 1: 1: 1: 1: 1] times, work last

55 sts as row 1 of panel C.
Row 2: Work first 55 sts as row **2** of panel C, (work next 8 sts as row **2** of panel D) 0 [0: 0: 1: 1: 1: 1: 1] times, work next 16 sts as row **2** of panel E, (K1, P1) 1 [3: 4: 2: 3: 5: 6: 7] times, K1 [0: 0: 1: 1: 0: 1: 1].
These 2 rows set the sts – patt panels with 3 [6: 8: 5: 7: 10: 13: 15] sts at side seam in moss st.
Working appropriate rows of panels and keeping sts correct as now set, complete to match left front, reversing shapings and working first row of front neck shaping as folls:

Shape front neck

Next row (RS): Break yarn and slip first 12 [12: 14: 13: 14: 15: 15: 15] sts onto a holder (for neckband), rejoin yarn and patt to end.
50 [53: 53: 59: 60: 62: 65: 67] sts.

LEFT SLEEVE

Using **3¾mm (US 5)** needles and yarn DOUBLE cast on
54 [54: 54: 54: 58: 62: 62: 62] sts.
Work in rib as given for back for 15 rows, inc 0 [0: 1: 1: 0: 0: 1: 1] st at each end of last row and ending with **WS** facing for next row.
54 [54: 56: 56: 58: 62: 64: 64] sts.
Change to **4½mm (US 7)** needles.
Now work in patt, placing cable panels as folls:
Row 1 (WS): P0 [0: 1: 1: 0: 0: 1: 1], (K1, P1) 5 [5: 5: 5: 6: 7: 7: 7] times, K1, work next 8 sts as row 1 of chart B – see panel/chart note, work next 16 sts as row 1 of chart A, work next 8 sts as row 1 of chart D – see panel/chart note, K1, (P1, K1) 5 [5: 5: 5: 6: 7: 7: 7] times, P0 [0: 1: 1: 0: 0: 1: 1].
Row 2: P0 [0: 1: 1: 0: 0: 1: 1], (K1, P1) 5 [5: 5: 5: 6: 7: 7: 7] times, P1, work next 8 sts as row 2 of chart D, work next 16 sts as row 2 of chart A, work next 8 sts as row 2 of chart B, P1, (P1, K1) 5 [5: 5: 5: 6: 7: 7: 7] times, P0 [0: 1: 1: 0: 0: 1: 1].
These 2 rows set the sts – patt panels at centre with 1 st in rev st st and moss st at each side.
Working appropriate rows of panels and keeping sts correct as now set, cont as folls:
Work 1 row, ending with **RS** facing for next row.
Inc 1 st at each end of next and every foll
6th [6th: 4th: 4th: 4th: 4th: 4th: 4th] row to
74 [74: 64: 76: 82: 86: 98: 98] sts, then on every foll
8th [8th: 6th: 6th: 6th: 6th: 6th: 6th] row until there are
86 [86: 96: 100: 104: 108: 114: 114] sts, taking inc sts into moss st.
Cont straight until sleeve meas 46 [46: 48: 48: 49: 49: 50: 50] cm, ending with **RS** facing for next row.

Shape top
Keeping patt correct, cast off 5 sts at beg of next 2 rows.
76 [76: 86: 90: 94: 98: 104: 104] sts.
Dec 1 st at each end of next and foll 5 alt rows, then on foll row, ending with **RS** facing for next row.
Cast off rem 62 [62: 72: 76: 80: 84: 90: 90] sts.

RIGHT SLEEVE
Work as given for left sleeve but replacing panel A with panel E throughout.

MAKING UP
Press as described on the information page.
Join both shoulder seams using mattress stitch.

Neckband
With **RS** facing, using **3¾mm (US 5)** needles and yarn DOUBLE, K across 12 [12: 14: 13: 14: 15: 15: 15] sts on right front holder, pick up and knit 15 [15: 15: 17: 17: 19: 19: 19] sts up right side of front neck, and 5 sts down right side of back neck, K across
36 [36: 40: 40: 42: 46: 46: 46] sts on back holder dec 1 st at centre, pick up and knit 5 sts up left side of back neck, and
15 [15: 15: 17: 17: 19: 19: 19] sts down left side of front neck, then K across
12 [12: 14: 13: 14: 15: 15: 15] sts on left front holder.
99 [99: 107: 109: 113: 123: 123: 123] sts.
Row 1 (WS): K1, *P1, K1, rep from * to end.
Row 2: K2, *P1, K1, rep from * to last st, K1.
These 2 rows form rib.
Cont in rib for a further 7 rows, ending with **RS** facing for next row.
Cast off in rib.

Button band
With **RS** facing, using **3¾mm (US 5)** needles and yarn DOUBLE, pick up and knit 129 [136: 143: 143: 143: 150: 150: 150] sts evenly up entire right front opening edge, from cast-on edge to top of neckband.
Beg with row 1, work in rib as given for neckband for 8 rows, ending with **RS** facing for next row.
Cast off in rib.

Buttonhole band
With **RS** facing, using **3¾mm (US 5)** needles and yarn DOUBLE, pick up and knit 129 [136: 143: 143: 143: 150: 150: 150] sts evenly down entire left front opening edge, from top of neckband to cast-on edge.
Beg with row 1, work in rib as given for neckband as folls:

Work 4 rows, ending with **WS** facing for next row.
Row 5 (WS): Rib 4, *cast off 2 sts (to make a buttonhole – cast on 2 sts over these cast-off sts on next row), rib until there are 15 [16: 17: 17: 17: 18: 18: 18] sts on right needle after cast-off, rep from * 6 times more, cast off 2 sts (to make 8th buttonhole – cast on 2 sts over these cast-off sts on next row), rib to end.
Work a further 3 rows, ending with **WS** facing for next row.
Next row (WS): Cast off in rib the first
120 [127: 134: 134: 134: 141: 141: 141] sts, rib rem 9 sts.
Working first and last sts of these 9 sts as a K st on every row and all other sts in rib, shape tab as folls:
Work 4 rows, ending with **RS** facing for next row.
Next row (RS): K2, P1, K1, yfwd (to make buttonhole for small button), K2tog, P1, K2.
Work 2 rows, ending with **WS** facing for next row.
Next row (WS): K1, P2tog, P1, K1, P1, P2tog tbl, K1. 7 sts.
Next row: K1, sl 1, K1, psso, P1, K2tog, K1. 5 sts.
Next row: K1, P3tog, K1. 3 sts.
Next row: Sl 1, K2tog, psso and fasten off.

See information page for finishing instructions, setting in sleeves using shallow set-in method, attaching buttons to button band and neck band to correspond with buttonhole in tab as shown in photograph.

PANEL A

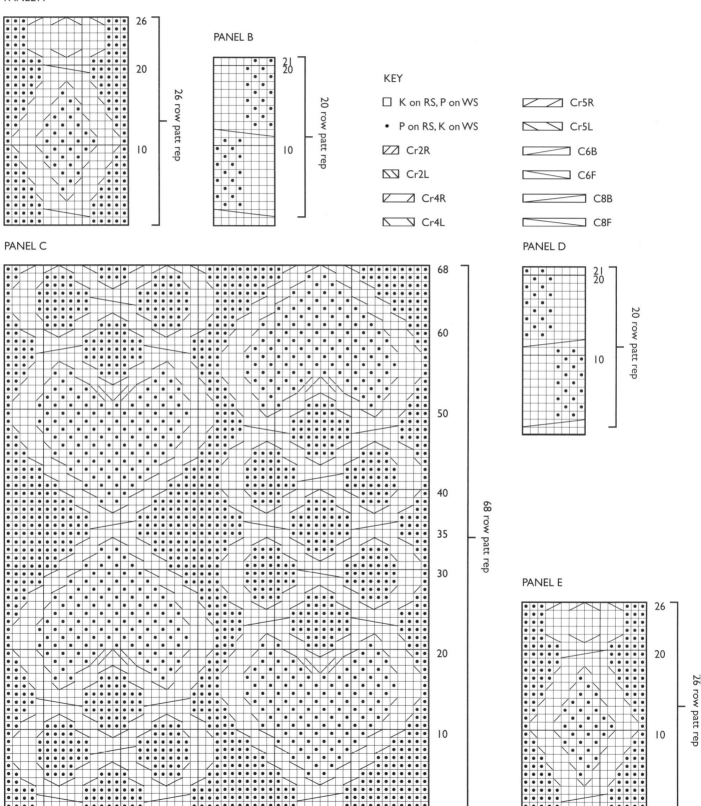

PANEL B

KEY

☐ K on RS, P on WS

• P on RS, K on WS

Cr2R

Cr2L

Cr4R

Cr4L

Cr5R

Cr5L

C6B

C6F

C8B

C8F

PANEL C

PANEL D

PANEL E

glenridding

Experience ●●●

To fit chest

	XS	S	M	L	XL	XXL	2XL	3XL	
	97-102	102-107	107-112	112-117	117-122	122-127	127-132	132-137	cm
	38-40	40-42	42-44	44-46	46-48	48-50	50-52	52-54	in

Marie Wallin British Breeds

A Ocean									
	6	6	7	7	8	8	9	9	x 25gm
B Silver Birch									
	5	5	6	6	6	7	7	7	x 25gm
C Eau de Nil									
	1	1	1	1	1	2	2	2	x 25gm
D Corncockle									
	2	2	2	2	2	3	3	3	x 25gm
E Wood									
	2	2	2	2	2	3	3	3	x 25gm
F Walnut									
	2	2	2	2	2	2	2	2	x 25gm
G Raw									
	2	2	2	2	2	2	3	3	x 25gm
H Storm									
	4	4	4	5	5	5	5	5	x 25gm
I Pale Oak									
	2	3	3	3	3	3	3	3	x 25gm
J Mallard									
	2	2	2	2	2	2	2	2	x 25gm

Needles

1 pair 2¾mm (no 12) (US 2) needles
1 pair 3mm (no 11) (US 2/3) needles
1 pair 3¼mm (no 10) (US 3) needles
2¾mm (no 12) (US 2) circular needle

Buttons

6 x TGB 2598 – 15mm from Textile Garden, see information page for contact details.

Tension

28 sts and 29 rows to 10 cm measured over patterned st st using 3¼mm (US 3) needles.

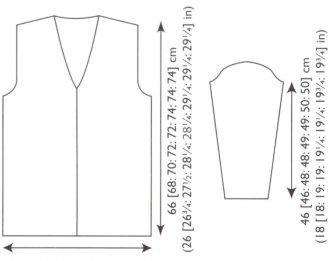

66 [68: 70: 72: 72: 74: 74: 74] cm
(26 [26¾: 27½: 28¼: 28¼: 29¼: 29¼: 29¼] in)

46 [46: 48: 48: 49: 49: 50: 50] cm
(18 [18: 19: 19: 19¼: 19¼: 19¾: 19¾] in)

52 [55.5: 57: 60.5: 62: 65.5: 68: 70.5] cm
(20½ [21¾: 22½: 23¾: 24½: 25¾: 26¾: 27¾] in)

Chart note: On the chart, the 73 row pattern repeat from rows 36 to 108 is an **odd** number of rows. On first and every following alternate row repeat of chart, work odd numbered rows as **RS** knit rows, reading chart from right to left. On second and every following alternate row repeat of chart, work odd numbered rows as **WS purl** rows, reading chart from left to right.

BACK

Using 2¾mm (US 2) needles and yarn A cast on
145 [155: 159: 169: 173: 183: 191: 197] sts.
Row 1 (RS): K1, *P1, K1, rep from * to end.
Row 2: P1, *K1, P1, rep from * to end.
These 2 rows form rib.
Join in yarn B.
Keeping rib correct and stranding yarn not in use across **WS** of work (this is back of work on **RS** rows, and front of work on **WS** rows), cont in 2-colour rib as folls:
Row 3 (RS): Using yarn A K1, *using yarn B P1, using yarn A K1, rep from * to end.
Row 4: Using yarn A P1, *using yarn B K1, using yarn A P1, rep from * to end.
Rows 5 to 22: As rows 3 and 4, 9 times.
Row 23: Using yarn A K1, *P1, K1, rep from * to end.
Row 24: Using yarn A, purl.
These 24 rows complete 2-colour rib.
Change to 3¼mm (US 3) needles.
Beg and ending rows as indicated, using the **fairisle** technique as described on the information page, working chart rows **1 to 35 once only** and then repeating chart rows **36 to 108 as a 73 row patt repeat 109 throughout (see chart note)**, cont in patt from chart, which is worked entirely in st st beg with a K row, as folls:
Cont straight until back meas 40 [42: 42: 43: 42: 43: 42: 42] cm, ending with **RS** facing for next row.
Shape armholes
Keeping patt correct, cast off 6 sts at beg of next 2 rows.
133 [143: 147: 157: 161: 171: 179: 185] sts.
(**Note:** Armhole shaping is **NOT** shown on chart.)
Dec 1 st at each end of next and foll 7 alt rows.
117 [127: 131: 141: 145: 155: 163: 169] sts.
Cont straight until armhole meas 23 [23: 25: 26: 27: 28: 29: 29] cm, ending with **RS** facing for next row.
Shape shoulders and back neck
Cast off 7 [8: 8: 9: 9: 9: 10: 11] sts at beg of next 2 rows.
103 [111: 115: 123: 127: 137: 143: 147] sts.
Next row (RS): Cast off 7 [8: 8: 9: 9: 10: 10: 11] sts, patt until there

are 25 [28: 28: 31: 32: 34: 37: 38] sts on right needle and turn, leaving rem sts on a holder.
Work each side of neck separately.
Dec 1 st at neck edge of next 4 rows **and at same time** cast off 7 [8: 8: 8: 9: 9: 10: 11] sts at beg of 2nd and foll alt row.
Work 1 row.
Cast off rem 7 [8: 8: 9: 10: 10: 11: 12] sts.
With **RS** facing, slip centre 39 [39: 43: 43: 45: 49: 49: 49] sts onto a holder (for front band), rejoin appropriate yarns and patt to end.
Complete to match first side, reversing shapings.

POCKET LININGS (make 2)
Using **3mm (US 2/3)** needles and yarn A cast on
36 [36: 38: 38: 40: 40: 42: 42] sts.
Beg with a K row, work in st st for 43 rows, ending with **WS** facing for next row.
Next row (WS): P5 [5: 5: 5: 6: 6: 6: 6], inc purlwise in next st, (P11 [11: 12: 12: 12: 12: 13: 13], inc purlwise in next st) twice, P6 [6: 6: 6: 7: 7: 7: 7]. 39 [39: 41: 41: 43: 43: 45: 45] sts.
Break yarn and leave sts on a holder.

LEFT FRONT
Using 2¾mm (US 2) needles and yarn A cast on
71 [77: 79: 83: 85: 91: 95: 97] sts.
Work rows 1 to 24 of 2-colour rib as given for back, inc 1 [0: 0: 1: 1: 0: 0: 1] st at end of last row and ending with **RS** facing for next row. 72 [77: 79: 84: 86: 91: 95: 98] sts.
Change to 3¼mm (US 3) needles.
Beg and ending rows as indicated, cont in patt from chart as folls:
Work 38 rows, ending with **RS** facing for next row.
Place pocket
Next row (RS): Using yarn E, K17 [19: 19: 22: 22: 24: 25: 27], slip next 39 [39: 41: 41: 43: 43: 45: 45] sts onto a holder (for pocket top) and, in their place, K across 39 [39: 41: 41: 43: 43: 45: 45] sts of first pocket lining, K rem 16 [19: 19: 21: 21: 24: 25: 26] sts.
Beg with chart row 40, now work in patt across all sts and cont as folls:
Cont straight until left front matches back to beg of armhole shaping, ending with **RS** facing for next row.
Shape armhole
Keeping patt correct, cast off 6 sts at beg of next row.
66 [71: 73: 78: 80: 85: 89: 92] sts.
Work 1 row.
Dec 1 st at armhole edge of next and foll 2 alt rows.
63 [68: 70: 75: 77: 82: 86: 89] sts.
Work 1 row, ending with **RS** facing for next row.

Shape front slope

Keeping patt correct, dec 1 st at end of next and foll
19 [19: 20: 19: 19: 22: 20: 20] alt rows, then on 3 [3: 4: 5: 6: 5: 7: 7] foll
4th rows **and at same time** dec 1 st at armhole edge of next and foll
4 alt rows. 35 [40: 40: 45: 46: 49: 53: 56] sts.
Cont straight until left front matches back to beg of shoulder shaping,
ending with **RS** facing for next row.

Shape shoulder

Keeping patt correct, cast off 7 [8: 8: 9: 9: 9: 10: 11] sts at beg of next
and foll 3 [3: 3: 3: 3: 0: 1: 3] alt rows, then – [-: -: -: -: 10: 11: -] sts at
beg of foll – [-: -: -: -: 3: 2: -] alt rows.
Work 1 row.
Cast off rem 7 [8: 8: 9: 10: 10: 11: 12] sts.

RIGHT FRONT

Using 2¾mm (US 2) needles and yarn A cast on
71 [77: 79: 83: 85: 91: 95: 97] sts.
Work rows 1 to 24 of 2-colour rib as given for back, inc
1 [0: 0: 1: 1: 0: 0: 1] st at beg of last row and ending with **RS** facing for
next row. 72 [77: 79: 84: 86: 91: 95: 98] sts.
Change to 3¼mm (US 3) needles.
Beg and ending rows as indicated, cont in patt from chart as folls:
Work 38 rows, ending with **RS** facing for next row.

Place pocket

Next row (RS): Using yarn E, K16 [19: 19: 21: 21: 24: 25: 26], slip next
39 [39: 41: 41: 43: 43: 45: 45] sts onto a holder (for pocket top) and, in
their place, K across
39 [39: 41: 41: 43: 43: 45: 45] sts of second pocket lining, K rem
17 [19: 19: 22: 22: 24: 25: 27] sts.
Beg with chart row 40, now work in patt across all sts and complete
to match left front, reversing shapings.

SLEEVES

Using 2¾mm (US 2) needles and yarn A cast on
61 [61: 65: 65: 67: 71: 73: 73] sts.
Work rows 1 to 24 of 2-colour rib as given for back, ending with **RS**
facing for next row.
Change to 3¼mm (US 3) needles.
Beg and ending rows as indicated, cont in patt from chart as folls:
Inc 1 st at each end of 3rd and every foll alt row to
83 [83: 97: 109: 113: 121: 127: 127] sts, then on every foll 4th row until
there are 123 [123: 135: 141: 145: 151: 157: 157] sts, taking inc sts into patt.
(**Note:** Sleeve shaping is only shown on chart for first 40 rows.)
Cont straight until sleeve meas 46 [46: 48: 48: 49: 49: 50: 50] cm,
ending with **RS** facing for next row.

Shape top

Keeping patt correct, cast off 6 sts at beg of next 2 rows.
111 [111: 123: 129: 133: 139: 145: 145] sts.
Dec 1 st at each end of next and foll 6 alt rows, then on foll row,
ending with **RS** facing for next row.
Cast off rem 95 [95: 107: 113: 117: 123: 129: 129] sts.

MAKING UP

Press as described on the information page.
Join both shoulder seams using mattress stitch.

Front band

With **RS** facing, using 2¾mm (US 2) circular needle and yarn A, beg
and ending at front cast-on edges, pick up and knit
123 [128: 128: 133: 128: 133: 128: 128] sts up right front opening edge
to beg of front slope shaping, 58 [58: 64: 66: 70: 71: 76: 76] sts up
right front slope, and 5 sts down right side of back neck, K across
39 [39: 43: 43: 45: 49: 49: 49] sts on back holder, then pick up and knit
5 sts up left side of back neck, 58 [58: 64: 66: 70: 71: 76: 76] sts down
left front slope to beg of front slope shaping, and
123 [128: 128: 133: 128: 133: 128: 128] sts down left front opening
edge. 411 [421: 437: 451: 451: 467: 467: 467] sts.
Join in yarn B.
Beg with row 4, now work in 2-colour rib as given for back as folls:
Work 5 rows, ending with **RS** facing for next row.
Row 6 (RS): Rib to last 121 [126: 126: 131: 126: 131: 126: 126] sts, *yrn,
work 2 tog (to make a buttonhole), rib 21 [22: 22: 23: 22: 23: 22: 22],
rep from * 4 times more, yrn, work 2 tog (to make 6th buttonhole),
rib 4.
Work in 2-colour rib for a further 4 rows, ending with **WS** facing for
next row.
Break off yarn B and cont using yarn A **only** as folls:
Work in rib for a further 2 rows, ending with **WS** facing for next row.
Cast off in rib (on **WS**).

Pocket tops (both alike)

With **RS** facing, slip 39 [39: 41: 41: 43: 43: 45: 45] sts from pocket
holder onto 2¾mm (US 2) needles, rejoin yarn A with **RS** facing and
K to end.
Join in yarn B.
Beg with row 4, now work in 2-colour rib as given for back as folls:
Work 4 rows, ending with **WS** facing for next row.
Break off yarn B and cont using yarn A only as folls:
Work in rib for a further 2 rows, ending with **WS** facing for next row.
Cast off in rib (on **WS**).
See information page for finishing instructions, setting in sleeves using
shallow set-in method.

■ A. Ocean   □ B. Silver Birch   • C. Eau de Nil   ○ D. Corncockle   ▲ E. Wood   ▼ F. Walnut   △ G. Raw   ● H. Storm   ✕ I. Pale Oak   ◢ J. Mallard

3XL 2XL XXL   XL L   M S   XS

2XL XL XS
3XL   S
XXL   M
      L
SLEEVES

cumbria

Left Front

XS
S
M
L
XL
2XL
3XL
XXL

SLEEVES

XS   S   M   L   XL   XXL   2XL   3XL

73 row patt rep

108
100
90
80
70
60
50
40
30
20
10

ight
ront

cumbria

93

keris

Experience ●●●

To fit bust

	S	M	L	XL	XXL	2XL	3XL	
	81-86	91-97	102-107	112-117	122-127	132-137	142-147	cm
	32-34	36-38	40-42	44-46	48-50	52-54	56-58	in

Marie Wallin British Breeds

	S	M	L	XL	XXL	2XL	3XL	
A Silver Birch	3	4	4	4	5	5	6	× 25gm
B Mallard	1	2	2	2	2	2	2	× 25gm
C Blossom	3	3	3	4	4	4	5	× 25gm
D Dark Apple	2	2	2	2	3	3	3	× 25gm
E Raw	1	1	1	1	1	2	2	× 25gm
F Walnut	1	1	2	2	2	2	2	× 25gm
G Dahlia	1	1	1	1	1	2	2	× 25gm
H Quince	1	1	1	2	2	2	2	× 25gm
I Rose	2	2	2	2	2	3	3	× 25gm
J Eau de Nil	1	1	1	1	1	1	2	× 25gm
K Lime Flower	1	1	1	1	1	1	2	× 25gm
L Evergreen	1	1	1	1	1	1	2	× 25gm
M Thistle	1	2	2	2	2	2	2	× 25gm
N Pale Oak	1	1	1	1	1	1	1	× 25gm

Needles

1 pair **2¾mm** (no 12) (US 2) needles
1 pair **3¼mm** (no 10) (US 3) needles

Tension

28 sts and 29 rows to 10 cm measured over patterned st st using **3¼mm (US 3)** needles.

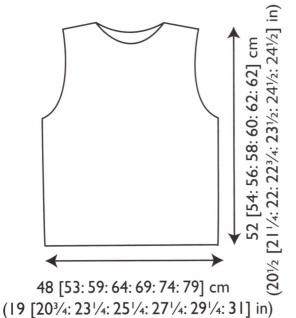

52 [54: 56: 58: 60: 62: 62] cm
(20½ [21¼: 22: 22¾: 23½: 24½: 24½] in)

48 [53: 59: 64: 69: 74: 79] cm
(19 [20¾: 23¼: 25¼: 27¼: 29¼: 31] in)

Chart note: Chart pattern repeat is an **odd** number of rows. On first rep of chart, work odd numbered rows as **RS** knit rows, reading chart from right to left. On second rep of chart, work odd numbered rows as **WS purl** rows, reading chart from left to right.

BACK

Using **2¾mm (US 2)** needles and yarn A cast on 135 [149: 165: 179: 193: 207: 221] sts.
Row 1 (RS): K1, *P1, K1, rep from * to end.
Row 2: P1, *K1, P1, rep from * to end.
These 2 rows form rib.
Work in rib for a further 4 rows, ending with **RS** facing for next row.
Change to **3¼mm (US 3)** needles.
Beg and ending rows as indicated, using the **fairisle** technique as described on the information page and repeating the 89 row patt repeat throughout (see chart note), cont in patt from chart, which is worked entirely in st st beg with a K row, as folls:
Cont straight until back meas 31 [32: 33: 34: 35: 36: 35] cm, ending with **RS** facing for next row.

Shape armholes

Keeping patt correct, cast off 7 [8: 9: 10: 11: 12: 13] sts at beg of next 2 rows. 121 [133: 147: 159: 171: 183: 195] sts.
(**Note:** Armhole shaping is **NOT** shown on chart.)
Dec 1 st at each end of next 7 [7: 9: 9: 11: 11: 11] rows, then on foll 5 [8: 9: 11: 10: 11: 11] alt rows, then on foll 4th row.
95 [101: 109: 117: 127: 137: 149] sts.
Cont straight until armhole meas 18 [19: 20: 21: 22: 23: 24] cm, ending with **RS** facing for next row.

Shape shoulders and back neck

Cast off 4 [5: 5: 6: 7: 8: 9] sts at beg of next 2 rows.
87 [91: 99: 105: 113: 121: 131] sts.
Next row (RS): Cast off 4 [5: 5: 6: 7: 8: 9] sts, patt until there are 18 [19: 22: 24: 25: 28: 31] sts on right needle and turn, leaving rem sts on a holder.
Work each side of neck separately.
Dec 1 st at neck edge of next 4 rows **and at same time** cast off 4 [5: 6: 6: 7: 8: 9] sts at beg of 2nd row, then 5 [5: 6: 7: 7: 8: 9] sts at beg of foll alt row.
Work 1 row.
Cast off rem 5 [5: 6: 7: 7: 8: 9] sts.
With **RS** facing, slip centre 43 [43: 45: 45: 49: 49: 51] sts onto a holder (for neckband), rejoin appropriate yarns and patt to end.
Complete to match first side, reversing shapings.

FRONT

Work as given for back until 10 [10: 12: 12: 14: 16: 16] rows less have been worked than on back to beg of shoulder shaping, ending with **RS** facing for next row.

Shape front neck

Next row (RS): Patt 32 [35: 39: 43: 47: 53: 58] sts and turn, leaving rem sts on a holder.
Work each side of neck separately.
Keeping patt correct, dec 1 st at neck edge of next 8 rows, then on foll 0 [0: 1: 1: 2: 3: 3] alt rows.
24 [27: 30: 34: 37: 42: 47] sts.
Work 1 row, ending with **RS** facing for next row.

Shape shoulder

Cast off 4 [5: 5: 6: 7: 8: 9] sts at beg of next and foll 2 [3: 1: 2: 3: 3: 3] alt rows, then 5 [-: 6: 7: -: -: -] sts at beg of foll 1 [-: 2: 1: -: -: -] alt rows **and at same time** dec 1 st at neck edge of next and foll alt row.
Work 1 row.
Cast off rem 5 [5: 6: 7: 7: 8: 9] sts.
With **RS** facing, slip centre 31 [31: 31: 31: 33: 31: 33] sts onto a holder (for neckband), rejoin appropriate yarns and patt to end.
Complete to match first side, reversing shapings.

MAKING UP

Press as described on the information page.
Join right shoulder seam using mattress stitch.

Neckband

With **RS** facing, using **2¾mm (US 2)** needles and yarn A, pick up and knit 20 [20: 22: 22: 24: 26: 26] sts down left side of front neck, K across 31 [31: 31: 31: 33: 31: 33] sts on front holder, pick up and knit 20 [20: 22: 22: 24: 26: 26] sts up right side of front neck, and 5 sts down right side of back neck, K across 43 [43: 45: 45: 49: 49: 51] sts on back holder dec 1 st at centre, then pick up and knit 5 sts up left side of back neck.
123 [123: 129: 129: 139: 141: 145] sts.
Beg with row 2, work in rib as given for back for 4 rows, ending with **WS** facing for next row.
Cast off in rib (on **WS**).
Join left shoulder and neckband seam.

Armhole borders (both alike)

With **RS** facing, using **2¾mm (US 2)** needles and yarn A, pick up and knit 115 [123: 131: 137: 145: 153: 161] sts evenly all round armhole edge.
Beg with row 2, work in rib as given for back for 4 rows, ending with **WS** facing for next row.
Cast off in rib (on **WS**).
See information page for finishing instructions.

KEY

☐ A. Silver Birch   ╱ E. Raw   ✕ J. Eau de Nil

■ B. Mallard   ▼ F. Walnut   ○ K. Lime Flower

· C. Blossom   ◖ G. Dahlia   ▬ L. Evergreen

● D. Dark Apple   △ H. Quince   ◆ M. Thistle

    ▲ I. Rose   ⋀ N. Pale Oak

Tip!
This chart has been split over two pages. Using the PDF (see info page), print out both halves and join them together

3XL   2XL   XXL   XL   L   M   S

89 row patt rep

S   M   L   XL   XXL   2XL   3XL

lingmoor

Experience ●●●

To fit bust

	S	M	L	XL	XXL	2XL	3XL	
	81-86	91-97	102-107	112-117	122-127	132-137	142-147	cm
	32-34	36-38	40-42	44-46	48-50	52-54	56-58	in

Marie Wallin British Breeds

	S	M	L	XL	XXL	2XL	3XL	
A Silver Birch	4	5	5	6	6	7	7	× 25gm
B Mallard	2	2	3	3	3	3	3	× 25gm
C Chestnut	3	3	3	3	3	4	4	× 25gm
D Eau de Nil	2	2	2	2	3	3	3	× 25gm
E Blossom	2	2	2	2	2	2	3	× 25gm
F Rose	1	2	2	2	2	2	2	× 25gm
G Lime Flower	2	2	2	2	3	3	3	× 25gm
H Dark Apple	2	2	2	2	2	2	2	× 25gm
I Walnut	2	2	3	3	3	3	3	× 25gm
J Wood	2	2	2	2	3	3	3	× 25gm
K Quince	1	1	2	2	2	2	2	× 25gm
L Foxglove	1	2	2	2	2	2	2	× 25gm
M Russet	2	2	2	2	3	3	3	× 25gm
N Pale Oak	1	2	2	2	2	2	2	× 25gm

Needles

1 pair 2¾mm (no 12) (US 2) needles
1 pair 3¼mm (no 10) (US 3) needles

Tension

28 sts and 29 rows to 10 cm measured over patterned st st using 3¼mm (US 3) needles.

68 [70: 72: 73: 74: 75: 76] cm
(26¾ [27½: 28¼: 28¾: 29¼: 29½: 30] in)

44 [45: 46: 46: 46: 46: 46] cm
(17½ [17¾: 18: 18: 18: 18: 18] in)

46 [51: 57: 62: 67: 72: 77] cm
(18 [20: 22½: 24½: 26½: 28¼: 30¼] in)

BACK

Using 2¾mm (US 2) needles and yarn A cast on
129 [143: 159: 173: 187: 201: 215] sts.
Row 1 (RS): K1, *P1, K1, rep from * to end.
Row 2: P1, *K1, P1, rep from * to end.
These 2 rows form rib.
Join in yarn B.
Keeping yarn not in use at **WS** of work (this is back of work on **RS**
rows, and front of work on **WS** rows), now work in 2-colour rib as folls:
Row 3 (RS): Using yarn A K1, *using yarn B P1, using yarn A K1, rep
from * to end.
Row 4: Using yarn A P1, *using yarn B K1, using yarn A P1, rep from *
to end.
Rep last 2 rows until rib meas 3.5 cm, ending with **RS** facing for next
row.
Break off yarn B.
Using yarn A **only**, work in rib for a further 2 rows, ending with **RS**
facing for next row.
Change to 3¼mm (US 3) needles.**
Beg and ending rows as indicated, using the **fairisle** technique as
described on the information page and repeating the 186 row patt
repeat throughout, cont in patt from chart, which is worked entirely
in st st beg with a K row, as folls:
Cont straight until back meas 47 [48: 49: 49: 49: 49: 49] cm, ending
with **RS** facing for next row.

Shape armholes

Keeping patt correct, cast off 6 [7: 8: 9: 10: 11: 12] sts at beg of next
2 rows. 117 [129: 143: 155: 167: 179: 191] sts. (**Note:** Armhole shaping
is **NOT** shown on chart.)
Dec 1 st at each end of next 5 [7: 7: 9: 9: 11: 11] rows, then on foll
5 [6: 9: 9: 10: 9: 9] alt rows, then on foll 4th row.
95 [101: 109: 117: 127: 137: 149] sts.
Cont straight until armhole meas 18 [19: 20: 21: 22: 23: 24] cm, ending
with **RS** facing for next row.

Shape shoulders and back neck

Cast off 3 [4: 5: 5: 6: 7: 8] sts at beg of next 2 rows.
89 [93: 99: 107: 115: 123: 133] sts.
Next row (RS): Cast off 4 [4: 5: 6: 6: 7: 8] sts, patt until there are
16 [18: 19: 22: 25: 28: 31] sts on right needle and turn, leaving rem sts
on a holder.
Work each side of neck separately.
Keeping patt correct, dec 1 st at neck edge of next 4 rows **and at
same time** cast off 4 [4: 5: 6: 7: 8: 9] sts at beg of 2nd row, then
4 [5: 5: 6: 7: 8: 9] sts at beg of foll alt row.

Work 1 row.
Cast off rem 4 [5: 5: 6: 7: 8: 9] sts.
With **RS** facing, slip centre 49 [49: 51: 51: 53: 53: 55] sts onto a holder
(for neckband), rejoin appropriate yarns and patt to end.
Complete to match first side, reversing shapings.

FRONT

Work as given for back until 4 [4: 6: 6: 8: 10: 10] rows less have been
worked than on back to beg of shoulder shaping, ending with **RS**
facing for next row.

Shape front neck

Next row (RS): Patt 26 [29: 33: 37: 42: 48: 53] sts and turn, leaving
rem sts on a holder.
Work each side of neck separately.
Keeping patt correct, dec 1 st at neck edge of next 3 [3: 5: 5: 6: 6: 6]
rows, then on foll 0 [0: 0: 0: 0: 1: 1] alt rows.
23 [26: 28: 32: 36: 41: 46] sts.
Work 0 [0: 0: 0: 1: 1: 1] row, ending with **RS** facing for next row.

Shape shoulder

Keeping patt correct, cast off 3 [4: 5: 5: 6: 7: 8] sts at beg of next and
foll 0 [2: 3: 0: 1: 1: 1] alt rows, then 4 [5: -: 6: 7: 8: 9] sts at beg of foll
3 [1: -: 3: 2: 2: 2] alt rows **and at same time** dec 1 st at neck edge of
next 3 [3: 1: 1: 1: 1: 1] rows, then on foll 1 [1: 2: 2: 2: 2: 2] alt rows.
Work 1 row.
Cast off rem 4 [5: 5: 6: 7: 8: 9] sts.
With **RS** facing, slip centre 43 [43: 43: 43: 43: 41: 43] sts onto a holder
(for neckband), rejoin appropriate yarns and patt to end.
Complete to match first side, reversing shapings.

SLEEVES

Using 2¾mm (US 2) needles and yarn A cast on
57 [59: 61: 61: 65: 65: 67] sts.
Work as given for back from ** to **.
Beg and ending rows as indicated and **beg with chart row 7** cont in
patt from chart as folls:
Inc 1 st at each end of 3rd and every foll 4th row until there are
81 [87: 91: 103: 107: 119: 123] sts, then on 9 [8: 8: 4: 4: 0: 0] foll 6th
rows, taking inc sts into patt.
99 [103: 107: 111: 115: 119: 123] sts.
(**Note:** Sleeve shaping is only shown on chart for first 40 rows.)
Cont straight until sleeve meas approx
44 [45: 46: 46: 46: 46: 46] cm, ending after same chart row as on back
to beg of armhole shaping and with **RS** facing for next row.

BOTTOM SECTIONS OF BODY CHART

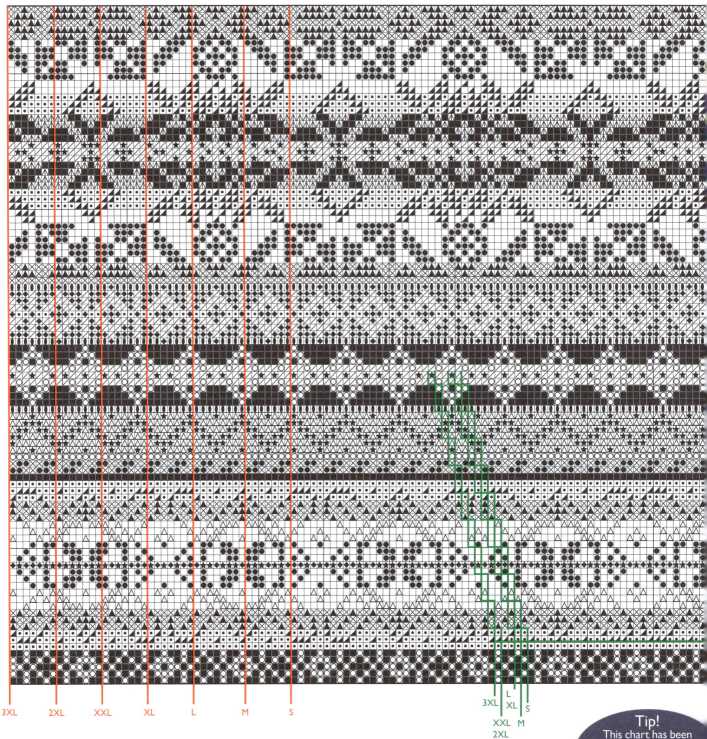

3XL 2XL XXL XL L M S

3XL XXL 2XL L XL XXL M S

Shape top

Keeping patt correct, cast off 6 [7: 8: 9: 10: 11: 12] sts at beg of next 2 rows. 87 [89: 91: 93: 95: 97: 99] sts.

Dec 1 st at each end of next 7 rows, then on every foll alt row until 61 sts rem, then on foll 11 rows, ending with **RS** facing for next row. 39 sts.

Cast off 7 sts at beg of next 2 rows.

Cast off rem 25 sts.

MAKING UP

Press as described on the information page.

Join right shoulder seam using mattress stitch.

Neckband

With **RS** facing and using **2¾mm (US 2)** needles, pick up and knit 11 [11: 13: 13: 15: 17: 17] sts down left side of front neck, K across 43 [43: 43: 43: 43: 41: 43] sts on front holder, pick up and knit 11 [11: 13: 13: 15: 17: 17] sts up right side of front neck, and 5 sts down

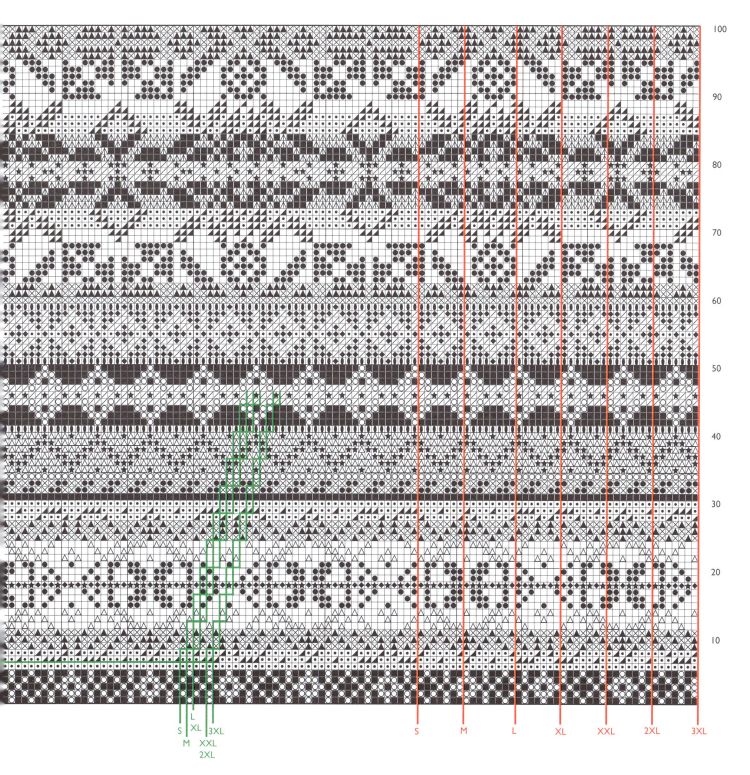

right side of back neck, K across

49 [49: 51: 51: 53: 53: 55] sts on back holder dec 1 st at centre, then pick up and knit 5 sts up left side of back neck.

123 [123: 129: 129: 135: 137: 141] sts.

Join in yarn B.

Row 1 (WS): Using yarn A P1, *using yarn B K1, using yarn A P1, rep from * to end.

Row 2: Using yarn A K1, *using yarn B P1, using yarn A K1, rep from *

to end.

Rep last 2 rows once more.

Break off yarn B.

Using yarn A **only**, work in rib for a further 2 rows, ending with **WS** facing for next row.

Cast off in rib (on **WS**).

See information page for finishing instructions, setting in sleeves using the set-in method.

TOP SECTIONS OF BODY CHART

KEY

□ A. Silver Birch   ■ C. Chestnut   ◢ F. Rose   △ I. Walnut   ◖ L. Foxglove
● B. Mallard   ○ D. Eau de Nil   × G. Lime Flower   ◆ J. Wood   ╱ M. Russet
    • E. Blossom   ▲ H. Dark Apple   ★ K. Quince   ⋀ N. Pale Oak

Tip!
This chart has been split over four pages. Using the PDF (see info page), print out all parts and join them together

3XL   2XL   XXL   XL   L   M   S

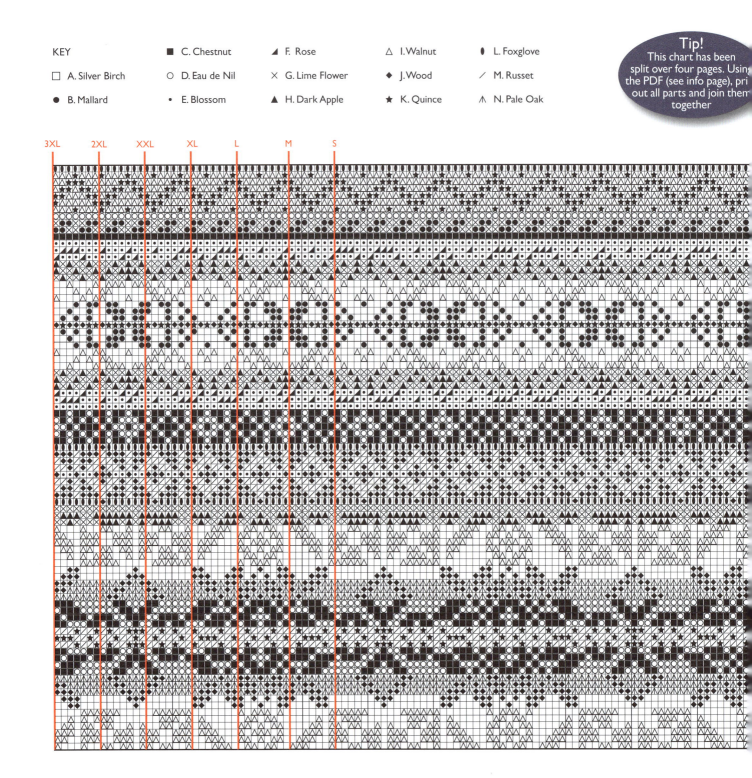

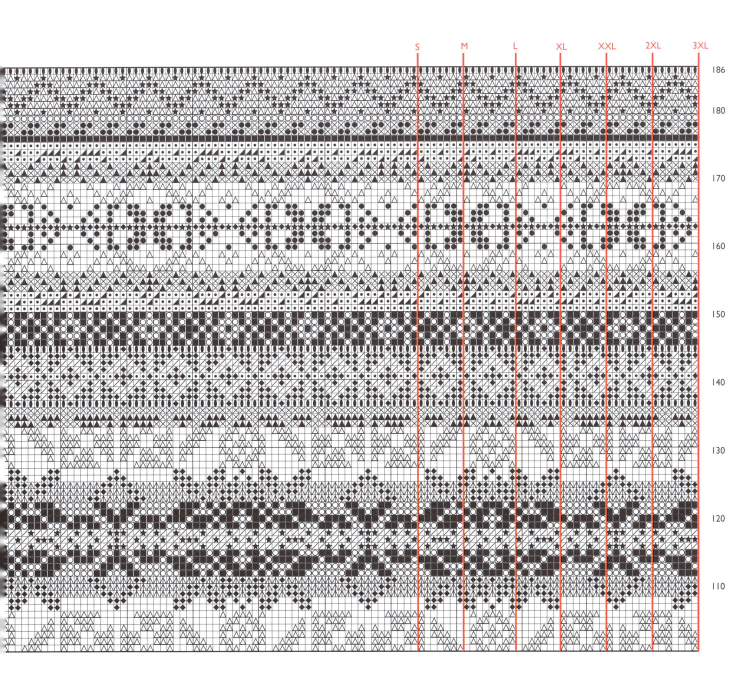

rydal

Experience ●●○

To fit bust

	S	M	L	XL	XXL	2XL	3XL	
	81-86	91-97	102-107	112-117	122-127	132-137	142-147	cm
	32-34	36-38	40-42	44-46	48-50	52-54	56-58	in

Marie Wallin British Breeds

	S	M	L	XL	XXL	2XL	3XL	
A Silver Birch	2	2	3	3	3	3	3	× 25gm
B Dark Apple	I	I	I	I	I	I	I	× 25gm
C Pale Oak	3	3	3	4	4	4	4	× 25gm
D Walnut	I	I	I	I	I	I	I	× 25gm
E Thistle	I	I	I	I	I	I	I	× 25gm
F Blossom	3	3	3	4	4	4	4	× 25gm
G Rose	I	I	I	I	I	I	I	× 25gm
H Dahlia	I	I	I	I	I	I	I	× 25gm
I Quince	I	I	I	I	I	I	I	× 25gm
J Corncockle	2	2	2	3	3	3	3	× 25gm
K Mulberry	I	2	2	2	2	2	2	× 25gm
L Lime Flower	3	3	3	3	4	4	4	× 25gm
M Woad	I	I	I	I	2	2	2	× 25gm
N Chestnut	I	I	I	I	I	I	2	× 25gm
O Eau de Nil	2	2	2	2	3	3	3	× 25gm
P Seagrass	I	I	I	I	I	I	I	× 25gm

Needles

I pair 2¾mm (no 12) (US 2) needles
I pair 3¼mm (no 10) (US 3) needles
2¾mm (no 12) (US 2) circular needle
3¼mm (no 10) (US 3) circular needle
Set of 4 double-pointed 2¾mm (no 12) (US 2) needles
Set of 4 double-pointed 3¼mm (no 10) (US 3) needles

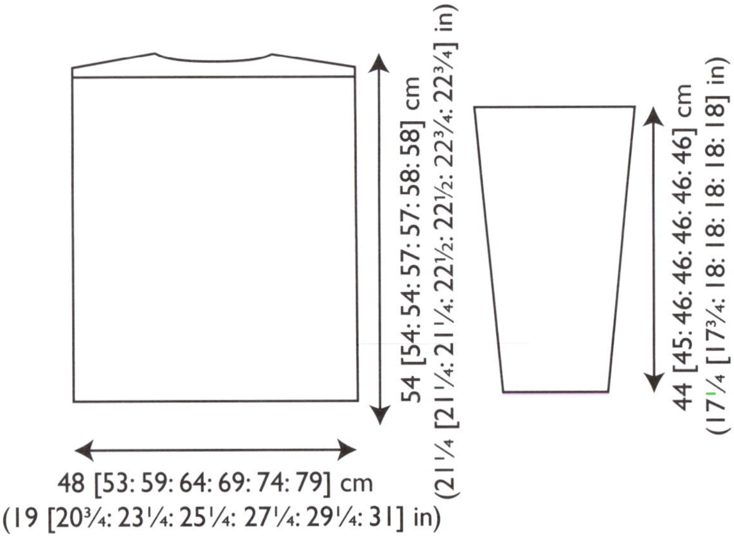

54 [54: 54: 57: 57: 58: 58] cm
(21¼ [21¼: 21¼: 22½: 22½: 22¾: 22¾] in)

44 [45: 46: 46: 46: 46] cm
(17¼ [17¾: 18: 18: 18: 18] in)

48 [53: 59: 64: 69: 74: 79] cm
(19 [20¾: 23¼: 25¼: 27¼: 29¼: 31] in)

Tension
28 sts and 29 rounds to 10 cm measured over patterned st st using 3¼mm (US 3) needles.

BODY (worked in one piece to armholes)
Using 2¾mm (US 2) circular needle and yarn C cast on
270 [298: 330: 358: 386: 414: 442] sts.
Taking care not to twist cast-on edge and placing a marker on first st of next round to denote beg and end of rounds, cont as folls:
Round 1 (RS): *K1, P1, rep from * to end.
This round forms the rib.
Using yarn C, work in rib for a further 3 rounds.
Joining in and breaking off colours as required, cont in rib in stripes as folls:
Rounds 5 to 8: Using yarn F.
Rounds 9 to 12: Using yarn J.
Rounds 13 to 16: Using yarn A.
Rounds 17 to 20: Using yarn O.
Rounds 21 to 24: Using yarn L.
Rounds 25 to 28: Using yarn C.
Rounds 5 to 28 form stripe sequence (of 4 rounds using each colour).
Work in rib in stripe sequence as now set for a further
20 [20: 20: 24: 24: 28: 28] rounds, ending after 4 rounds using yarn L [L: L: C: C: F: F].
Change to 3¼mm (US 3) circular needle.
Beg and ending rounds as indicated and using the **fairisle** technique as described on the information page, cont in patt from body chart for appropriate size being knitted (this is 111 rounds for sizes S, M and L, and 117 rounds for sizes XL, XXL, 2XL and 3XL), which is worked mainly in st st (K every round), as folls:
Round 1 (RS): (Work next 135 [149: 165: 179: 193: 207: 221] sts as round 1 of appropriate body chart repeating the 24 st patt rep 5 [6: 6: 7: 8: 8: 9] times) twice.
This round sets the sts.
Cont as now set until chart round 65 [62: 59: 62: 59: 56: 53] has been completed.
Remove marker.

Position armholes
Next round (RS): Using yarn L cast on and K 5 sts (for first part of first armhole steek), place marker on right needle, patt next 135 [149: 165: 179: 193: 207: 221] sts, place marker on right needle, turn and using yarn L cast on 9 sts (for second armhole steek), turn, place marker on right needle, patt next 135 [149: 165: 179: 193: 207: 221] sts, place marker on right needle, turn and cast on 4 sts (for second part of first armhole steek, turn.

This round sets the sts – 2 sets of 9 steek sts for armholes (with markers either side), work these steek sts in a vertical or birds eye patt of main and contrast colours and cont working all other sts all other sts in patt as set. (In areas of plain st st in one colour, work armhole steeks in the same colour).
Working steek sts as stated, cont straight until chart round 110 [110: 110: 116: 116: 116: 116] has been completed.
Next round: Cast off first 5 steek sts, patt next 135 [149: 165: 179: 193: 207: 221] sts and slip these sts onto a holder (for first shoulder and neck rib section), cast off next 9 steek sts, patt next 135 [149: 165: 179: 193: 207: 221] sts and slip these sts onto another holder (for second shoulder and neck rib section), cast off rem 4 sts.

Shape first shoulder and neck section
Slip first set of 135 [149: 165: 179: 193: 207: 221] sts onto 2¾mm (US 2) straight needles and now, working backwards and forwards in rows, not rounds, rejoin yarn C with **RS** facing and work first shoulder and neck section as folls:
Row 1 (RS): Knit.
Row 2: K1, *P1, K1, rep from * to end.
Row 3: P1, *K1, P1, rep from * to end.
Last 2 rows form rib.
Keeping rib correct and joining in and breaking off colours as required, now work in stripes as folls:
Using yarn C, work 1 more row, ending with **RS** facing for next row.
Using yarn F, work 4 rows.
Shape shoulders
Using yarn J, cast off 9 [11: 12: 14: 15: 17: 18] sts at beg of next 2 rows, then 9 [11: 12: 14: 16: 17: 19] sts at beg of foll 2 rows.
99 [105: 117: 123: 131: 139: 147] sts.
Using yarn A, cast off 9 [11: 13: 14: 16: 18: 19] sts at beg of next 2 rows, then 10 [11: 13: 15: 16: 18: 19] sts at beg of foll 2 rows, ending with **RS** facing for next row.
Cast off rem 61 [61: 65: 65: 67: 67: 71] sts in rib.

Shape second shoulder and neck section
Slip second set of 135 [149: 165: 179: 193: 207: 221] sts onto 2¾mm (US 2) straight needles and now, working backwards and forwards in rows, not rounds, rejoin yarn C with **RS** facing and work second shoulder and neck section to match first shoulder and neck section from row 1 to end.

SLEEVES
Following instructions in steeking feature, work and cut armhole

BODY CHART
SIZES S, M & L

24 st patt rep

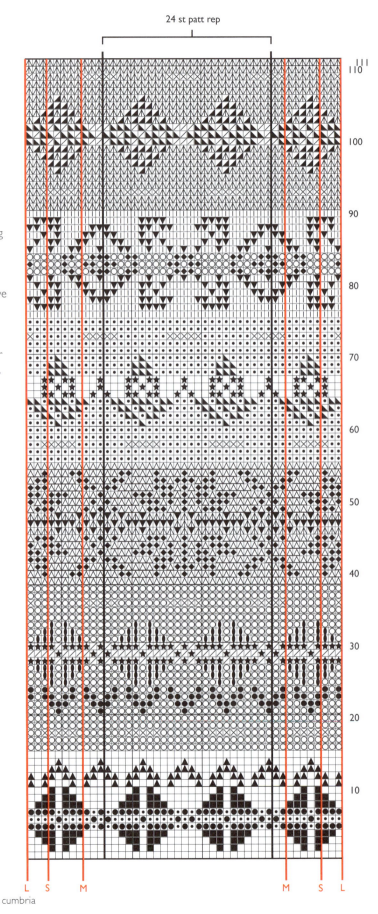

steeks. Join both shoulder seams, leaving final cast-off edge open (to form neck opening).

Using set of 4 double-pointed **3¼mm (US 3)** needles and yarn L, beg and ending at underarm point, pick up and knit
95 [101: 107: 113: 117: 123: 129] sts evenly all round armhole edge.
Distribute sts evenly over 3 of the 4 needles and, placing a marker between last picked-up st and first st of next round (to denote sleeve "seam"), cont as folls:

Beg and ending rounds as indicated, repeating the 24 st patt repeat twice around each round and using the **fairisle** technique as described on the information page, cont in patt from sleeve chart for appropriate size being knitted (this is 111 rounds for sizes S, M and L, and 117 rounds for sizes XL, XXL, 2XL and 3XL), which is worked mainly in st st (K every round), as folls:
Keeping patt correct, dec 1 st at each end of 3rd and
0 [0: 0: 0: 0: 0: 4] foll alt rounds, then on
1 [7: 13: 19: 19: 28: 26] foll 4th rounds, then on
17 [13: 9: 6: 6: 0: 0] foll 6th rounds.
57 [59: 61: 61: 65: 65: 67] sts.
Work 2 rounds, dec 1 st at end of last round and ending after chart round 111 [111: 111: 117: 117: 117: 117].
56 [58: 60: 60: 64: 64: 66] sts.
Break off yarns.
Change to **2¾mm (US 2)** double-pointed needles.
Joining in and breaking off colours as required and working in rib as given for body, now work in striped rib as folls:

Size L only
Using yarn F, knit one round, then work 3 rounds in rib.
Using C, work 4 rounds.

Size M only
Using yarn C, knit one round, then work 3 rounds in rib.

All sizes
Using yarn L, knit 1 [0: 0: 1: 1: 1: 1] round, then work
3 [4: 4: 3: 3: 3: 3] rounds in rib.
Using yarn O, work 4 rounds.
Using yarn A, work 4 rounds.
Using yarn J, work 4 rounds.
Using yarn F, work 4 rounds.
Using yarn C, work 4 rounds.
Cast off in rib.

MAKING UP
Press as described on the information page.
See information page for finishing instructions.

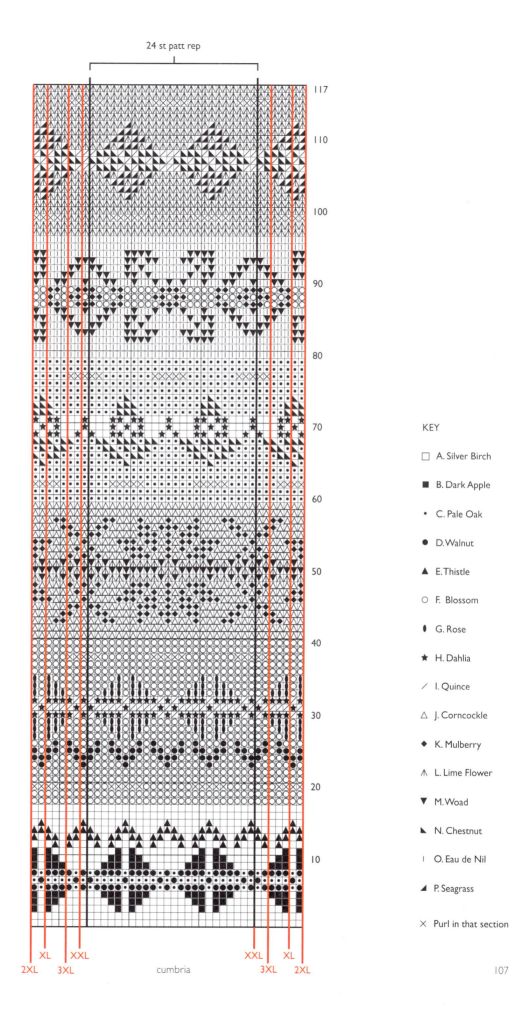

BODY CHART
SIZES XL, XXL, 2XL & 3XL

24 st patt rep

117
110
100
90
80
70
60
50
40
30
20
10

2XL XL XXL XXL XL 2XL
3XL cumbria 3XL

KEY

☐ A. Silver Birch

■ B. Dark Apple

· C. Pale Oak

● D. Walnut

▲ E. Thistle

○ F. Blossom

❥ G. Rose

★ H. Dahlia

╱ I. Quince

△ J. Corncockle

◆ K. Mulberry

Λ L. Lime Flower

▼ M. Woad

◣ N. Chestnut

| O. Eau de Nil

◢ P. Seagrass

✕ Purl in that section

24 st patt rep

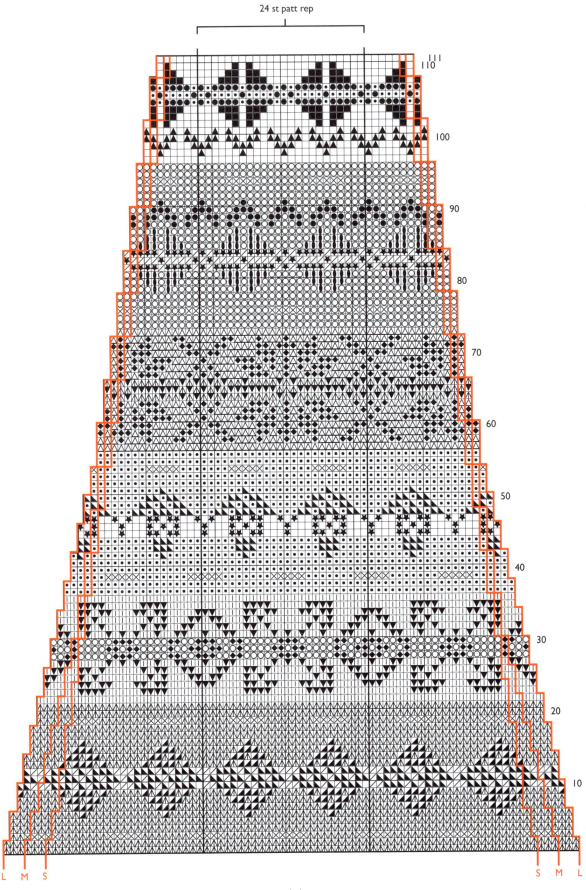

111
110

100

90

80

70

60

50

40

30

20

10

L M S

S M L

cumbria

SLEEVE CHART
SIZES XL, XXL, 2XL & 3XL

24 st patt rep

117
110
100
90
80
70
60
50
40
30
20
10

XL
XXL
XL
XL
2XL
XXL
3XL

cumbria

swaledale
scarf

Experience ●●○

Size
One size only

Marie Wallin British Breeds

A	Silver Birch	4 × 25gm
B	Mallard	1 × 25gm
C	Lime Flower	3 × 25gm
D	Ocean	2 × 25gm
E	Corncockle	1 × 25gm
F	Seagrass	2 × 25gm
G	Dahlia	1 × 25gm
H	Raw	2 × 25gm
I	Eau de Nil	1 × 25gm
J	Chestnut	2 × 25gm
K	Pale Oak	2 × 25gm
L	Evergreen	1 × 25gm
M	Mulberry	1 × 25gm
N	Willow	1 × 25gm
O	Wood	1 × 25gm

Needles
3¼mm (no 10) (US 3) circular needle no more than 50 cm long

Tension
29 sts and 30 rounds to 10 cm measured over patterned st st using 3¼mm (US 3) circular needle.

Finished size
Completed scarf measures 26 cm (10¼ in) wide when laid flat and 151.5 cm (59¾ in) long.

SCARF
Using 3¼mm (US 3) circular needle and yarn A cast on 150 sts.
Joining in and breaking off colours as required, using the **fairisle** technique as described on the information page and repeating the 30 st patt repeat 5 times around each round and repeating the 65 round patt repeat throughout, cont in patt from chart, which is worked entirely in st st (K every round), for 455 rounds (7 round patt repeats).
Cast off.

FINISHING
Press as described on the information page.
Sew in any loose ends on **WS** of scarf.
Smooth out the scarf so that it is flat and close the cast on edges together and the cast off edges together using mattress stitch.

30 st patt rep

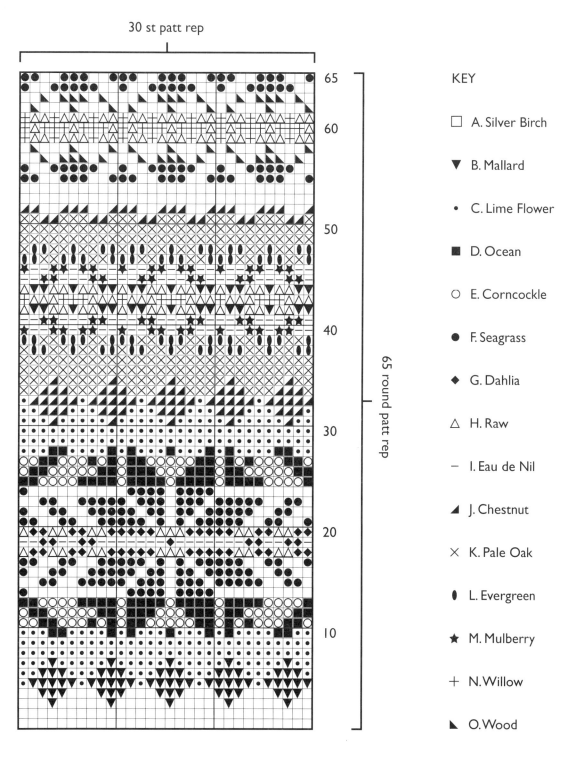

65

60

50

40

30

20

10

65 round patt rep

KEY

□ A. Silver Birch

▼ B. Mallard

• C. Lime Flower

■ D. Ocean

○ E. Corncockle

● F. Seagrass

◆ G. Dahlia

△ H. Raw

– I. Eau de Nil

◢ J. Chestnut

✕ K. Pale Oak

❘ L. Evergreen

★ M. Mulberry

+ N. Willow

◣ O. Wood

tarn tam

To fit average head
Women's 53 – 56 cm (20¾ – 22 in) **Men's** 59 – 62 cm (23¼ - 24½ in)

Marie Wallin British Breeds

Women's colourway			**Men's** colourway		
A	Raw	I × 25gm	A	Silver Birch	I × 25gm
B	Lime Flower	I × 25gm	B	Seagrass	I × 25gm
C	Evergreen	I × 25gm	C	Mulberry	I × 25gm
D	Quince	I × 25gm	D	Willow	I × 25gm
E	Dahlia	I × 25gm	E	Chestnut	I × 25gm
F	Eau de Nil	I × 25gm	F	Corncockle	I × 25gm
G	Blossom	I × 25gm	G	Eau de Nil	I × 25gm
H	Woad	I × 25gm	H	Wood	I × 25gm
I	Acer	I × 25gm	I	Ocean	I × 25gm
J	Thistle	I × 25gm	J	Walnut	I × 25gm
K	Foxglove	I × 25gm	K	Storm	I × 25gm

Needles
2¾mm (no 12) (US 2) circular needle or set of 4 double-pointed
2¾mm (no 12) (US 2) needles
3¼mm (no 10) (US 3) circular needle or set of 4 double-pointed
3¼mm (no 10) (US 3) needles

Tension
32 sts and 34 rounds to 10 cm measured over patterned st st using
3¼mm (US 3) needles.

TAM
Brim
Using 2¾mm (US 2) circular needle or double-pointed needles and
yarn A cast on 114 [130] sts.
Taking care not to twist cast-on edge, work in rounds as folls:
Round I (RS): *KI, PI, rep from * to end.
Place marker on first st of round just knitted to denote beg and end
of rounds.
Join in yarn I.
Keeping yarn not in use at **WS** of work, cont as folls:
Round 2: *Using yarn A KI, using yarn I PI, rep from * to end.
Rep round 2, 3 times more.
Break off yarn I and cont in yarn A **only**.
Next round: *KI, PI, rep from * to end.
Next round: K2tog, K to last 2 sts, K2tog. 112 [128] sts.
Break off yarn A.
Change to 3¼mm (US 3) circular needle or double-pointed needles.
Join in yarn B.
Increase round: Using yarn B, KI, *MI, K2, rep from * to last st, MI,
KI. 168 [192] sts.

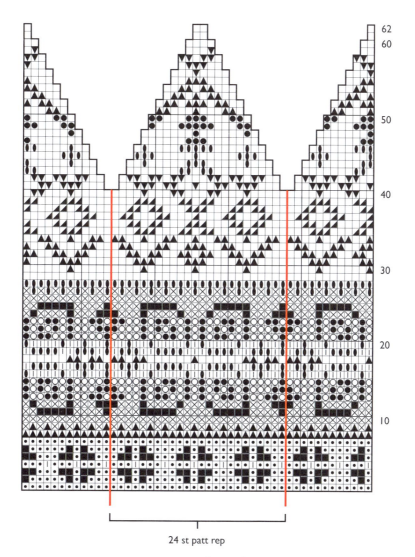

KEY – Women's

□	A. Raw
•	B. Lime Flower
■	C. Evergreen
I	D. Quince
▲	E. Dahlia
×	F. Eau de Nil
○	G. Blossom
●	H. Woad
❶	I. Acer
◢	J. Thistle
▼	K. Foxglove

KEY – Men's

□	A. Silver Birch
•	B. Seagrass
■	C. Mulberry
I	D. Willow
▲	E. Chestnut
×	F. Corncockle
○	G. Eau de Nil
●	H. Wood
❶	I. Ocean
◢	J. Walnut
▼	K. Storm

24 st patt rep

Work sides and crown of tam

Joining in and breaking off colours as required and using the **fairisle** technique as described on the information page, work from chart, which is worked entirely in st st (K every round) as folls:
Beg with **round 2** of chart, work the first 12 sts of chart, repeat the 24 st patt repeat 6 [7] times, then work the last 12 sts of chart on each round until round 62 has been completed, working decreases as indicated on the following rounds:
Round 41: (Patt 10 sts, sl 1, K2tog, psso, patt 11 sts) 7 [8] times. 154 [176] sts.
Round 43: (Patt 9 sts, sl 1, K2tog, psso, patt 10 sts) 7 [8] times. 140 [160] sts.
Round 45: (Patt 8 sts, sl 1, K2tog, psso, patt 9 sts) 7 [8] times. 126 [144] sts.
Round 47: (Patt 7 sts, sl 1, K2tog, psso, patt 8 sts) 7 [8] times. 112 [128] sts.
Round 49: (Patt 6 sts, sl 1, K2tog, psso, patt 7 sts) 7 [8] times. 98 [112] sts.

Round 51: (Patt 5 sts, sl 1, K2tog, psso, patt 6 sts) 7 [8] times. 84 [96] sts.
Round 53: (Patt 4 sts, sl 1, K2tog, psso, patt 5 sts) 7 [8] times. 70 [80] sts.
Round 55: (Patt 3 sts, sl 1, K2tog, psso, patt 4 sts) 7 [8] times. 56 [64] sts.
Round 57: (Patt 2 sts, sl 1, K2tog, psso, patt 3 sts) 7 [8] times. 42 [48] sts.
Round 59: (K1, sl 1, K2tog, psso, K2) 7 [8] times. 28 [32] sts.
Cont in yarn A only as folls:
Round 60: Knit.
Round 61: (sl 1, K2tog, psso, K1) 7 [8] times. 14 [16] sts.
Round 62: (K2tog) 7 [8] times. 7 [8] sts.
Break off yarn, thread through rem sts and draw up tightly.

FINISHING

Fasten off centre of tam on **WS**. Weave in any loose ends on **WS** of tam. Press tam gently on **WS** using a warm iron over a damp cloth.

cumbria

the langdale estate

The 35 acres of the beautiful Langdale Estate was one of the photography locations we used for Cumbria. Situated in the heart of the Lake District National Park and surrounded by stunning scenery and some of the finest hill walking in the country, the historic Langdale Estate offers visitors the chance to stay in luxury hotel and self-catering accommodation.

The Estate itself began life in the 17th Century as a small woollen mill, where wool from the surrounding area was processed in the wild waters of the Great Langdale beck. Then in the early 18th Century, the mill was converted into a gunpowder works! This local enterprise fed the demand from the growing number of local mines and quarries as well as exports to North America and South Africa. The gunpowder works closed in 1930, a victim of the depression and the arrival of more modern explosives, such as dynamite. From 1930 to 1981, the site was bought for conversion into a holiday resort. By the late 1930's, there was a small hotel, several cottages and a guest house! From 1981 to the present day, the Langdale Estate has been developed into a high quality luxury hotel and self catering accommodation and is the perfect base to explore this wonderful part of the Lake District.

www.langdale.co.uk

shacklabank farm

Shacklabank Farm is situated in the beautiful, wild Howgills of the Yorkshire Dales National Park and was used as one of our locations for Cumbria. It is home to my friend, Alison O'Neill, a rather special lady! Alison is simply someone that you instantly cannot help but like, her enthusiasm and passion for her sheep and her beloved Dales is very infectious.

Alison manages her sheep farm single handed with the help of her ever-faithful sheep dog, Shadow! As well as the demands of her beloved Rough Fell and Herdwick sheep, she finds time to run a bespoke tweed clothing and dog accessory business. Her lovely, twisted wool rope dog leads are a particular hit!

Surrounded by stunning scenery, Alison is also a fully qualified walking guide and takes great pleasure in sharing the beautiful landscapes of Cumbria and the Yorkshire Dales with people who want to explore this stunning area. She has even ventured further afield and now holds walking holidays in Scotland, in particular the Isles of Harris and Lewis in the Hebrides.

www.shepherdess.co.uk

cumbria

steeking

Steeking is a traditional method of turning a sweater knitted in the round into a cardigan. It can also be used to convert a flat knitted design into round knitting with the introduction of steek stitches where the side and armhole seams would be. To do this, extra stitches are knitted and then 'edged' before cutting. Steeking is most successful when the knitting yarn is 100% Wool as the 'sticky' fibres 'felt' together to help prevent any loose stitches from running. However, as my **British Breeds** yarn is worsted spun and therefore softer, I am recommending that for crochet steeking, you do an extra reinforcement of your steek with a line of hand or machine stitching before picking up any stitches.

Note: The images shown here show 9 steek stitches, but any odd number of stitches can be added instead, such as 5 or 7. Here the steek stitches are referred to in numbers **1** to **9**, from right to left. The steek stitch, ie: the one that is cut, is steek stitch **5** and is in the centre of the group of nine stitches. Here I explain how to steek using two methods, **crochet** and **machine stitch** steeking.

CROCHET STEEKING

1. When knitting a cardigan, the steek stitches for the centre front are worked by knitting the first 3, 4 or 5 steek stitches at the beginning of the round and the last 2, 3, or 4 steek stitches at the end. The new round and new colours are introduced on centre steek stitch of the front steek. When adding steek stitches for the side or armhole seams, the steek stitches are added, all together, either 5, 7 or 9 stitches and the steek stitch is the centre stitch of these 5, 7 or 9 stitches

It is very important that you do NOT weave any loose ends across the steek stitch, as this could cause the stitches to pull apart once cut. I tend to weave in the two new colours away from the steek as I knit the round from right to left. The two old colours I leave and sew in by hand from left to right after the knitting is complete. The steek stitches can be worked in a straight vertical line pattern or in a 'birdseye' pattern.

2. With **RS** facing and starting at the bottom of the work and using a fine crochet hook (eg. **2.50mm (US B1/C2)** hook) work one chain

stitch and start to work a double crochet **(dc) (sc)** into each stitch as follows: push the hook into the left hand leg of vertical steek stitch 4 and then into the right hand leg of vertical steek stitch 5 and complete a **dc (sc)** through both legs. Work a **dc (sc)** into each stitch all the way up the garment, work one ch. Break off the yarn. **Please refer to images a, b and c**

3. With **RS** facing rejoin the yarn and work in the same way down the garment from top to bottom, working a **dc (sc)** into the left hand leg of vertical steek stitch 5 and the right hand leg of vertical steek stitch 6. Break off yarn. **Please refer to image d**

4. Spread out the fabric and you will see a vertical line of horizontal stitches has appeared where vertical steek stitch 5 was, this is the cutting line. **Please refer to image e**

5. Carefully cut up this 'ladder' and the cut edges will disappear into the crochet 'edge' on either side of the fabric. **Please refer to image f**

6. The fabric is now ready to be folded back to the **WS** of the garment. This can be held in place by hand stitching with the fold along the 1st and 9th vertical steek stitch. The back of the steek can then be covered if preferred with a pretty woven ribbon or knitted strapping.

MACHINE STITCH STEEKING

If you do not like to crochet or you feel this method is too slow or difficult then try steeking by machine stitch reinforcement. The steek stitches are knitted in exactly the same way as described for the **crochet** method but leave the ends unwoven. This means that the ends will be loose at steek stitch 5. To prevent holes forming when knitting, just tie them together with a simple knot. All the ends and therefore the knots will be cut off when the steek is cut.

1. **DO NOT WEAVE or SEW** in the loose ends as these will be trimmed off later. **Please refer to image g**

2. Machine stitch or hand stitch using back stitch a double line up the centre of vertical steek stitches 2 and 8. **Please refer to image h**

3. Trim close to the double line of machine stitches on steek stitch 2 and 8, therefore cutting off all the loose ends. **Please refer to image i**

Finally, whichever method you choose you will soon realise that steeking is not difficult or scary at all! **Be brave!**

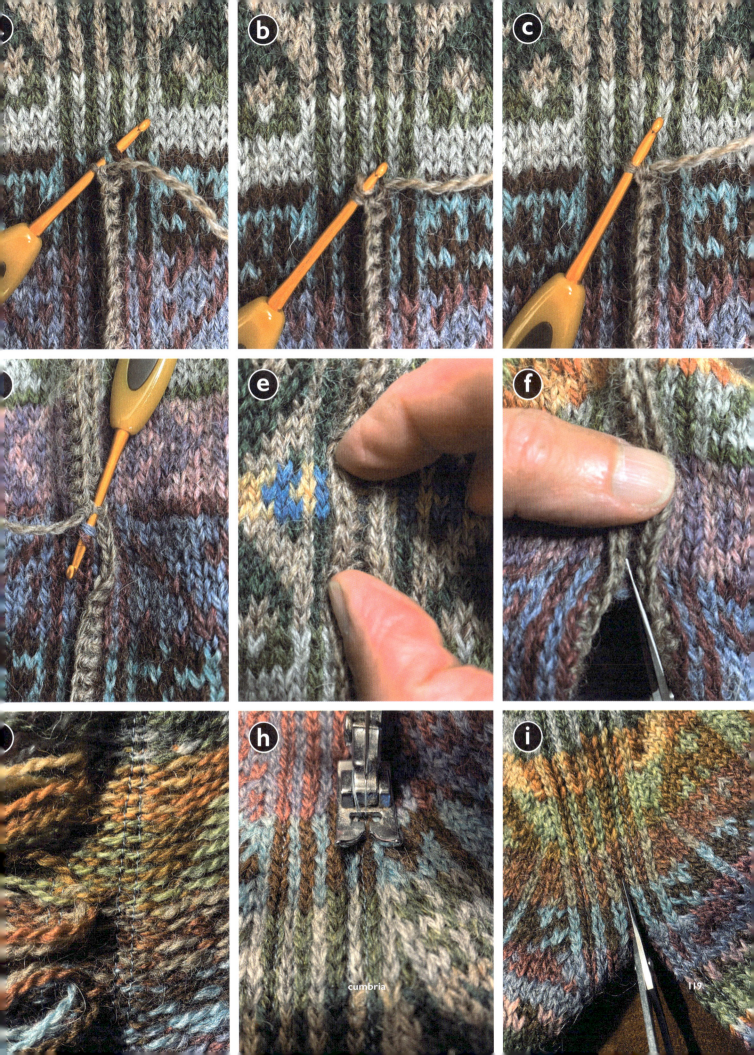

information

TENSION

Achieving the correct tension is one of the most important factors when knitting one of my designs. I cannot stress highly enough that you really do need to knit a tension square BEFORE you start to knit the garment. The tension stated on each of my patterns must be achieved to ensure that the garment fits correctly and that it matches the measurements stated on the size diagram. I recommend that you knit a square using the number of stitches and rows stated on the pattern tension plus 3 or 4 stitches and rows. To check your tension firstly steam your swatch using a WARM steam iron, hovering the iron just over the WS and letting the steam penetrate the fabric, this will allow the stitches in the swatch to fully relax. Then place the knitted square on a flat surface and mark out a 10cm square using pins as markers. Count the number of stitches and rows between the pins. If you have too many stitches, then your knitting is too tight, knit another square using a thicker needle. If you have too few stitches, then your knitting is too loose, knit another square using a thinner needle. It is also important to keep checking your tension whilst you are knitting your garment especially if you are returning to knit after leaving your work for a period of time.

SIZING

The patterns are written giving the instructions for the smallest size, for the other sizes work the figures in the brackets. The measurements stated on the size diagrams are the measurements of your finished garment AFTER pressing.

MODEL SIZE

Georgia is 5'8'' tall, is a standard UK size 8/10 and she is wearing the smallest size in each photograph. James is just under 6'4'' tall, is a standard size large and he is wearing size L in the photographs.

FAIRISLE - STRANDED COLOUR WORK

Fairisle is one of the main methods of adding colour into knitting. Fairisle is used when two colours are to be worked repeatedly along a row. The colour not being used is stranded fairly loosely behind the stitches being worked. It is very important not to pull this stranded yarn too tight as this will pucker your knitting and your stitch tension will be too tight, make sure to spread your stitches to ensure that they remain elastic. I would recommend that you carry the stranded or floating yarn over no more than 5 stitches when using a DK or 4 Ply yarn, and no more than 3 stitches when using an Aran or Chunky yarn. Weave the stranded colour under and over the colour being worked if you have to knit a colour over more than the recommended amount.

FINISHING

Finishing your garment beautifully is another important factor when making one of my designs. Good finishing will ensure that your garment fits correctly and washes and wears well. I urge you to spend time pressing and stitching your garment together, after all you've just spent a lot money and time knitting it using lovely yarns and the last thing you want to do is ruin it with bad finishing!

PRESSING

Firstly sew in any loose ends to the wrong side of the knitting. Block out each piece of knitting and then gently steam press on the WS on the knitting using a WARM steam iron. To do this, make sure that you hover the iron over the knitting and smooth flat with your hand. Do NOT put the full weight of the iron on the knitting even over a damp cloth as this will flatten it too much. If you are unsure about steaming your knitting then make sure that you use a protective cloth over your work before you hover over the steam iron. Pay particular attention to the sides or edges of each piece as this will make the sewing up both easier and neater. Take special care with the welts and cuffs of the knitting – if the garment is fitted then gently steam the ribs so that they fill out but remain elastic. If the garment is a boxy, straight shape then steam press out the ribs to correct width.

STITCHING

When stitching the pieces together, remember to match areas of colour, texture or pattern very carefully where they meet. I recommend that you use mattress stitch wherever possible, this stitch gives the neatest finish ensuring that the seam lays flat. Having knitted your pieces according to the pattern instructions, generally the shoulders seams of the front and back are joined together using mattress stitch. For a sweater knitted in pieces, only one shoulder seam is joined before working the neck trim. For a cardigan knitted in pieces, both shoulder seams are joined before working the edgings and neck trim. Work the neck trim and edging according to the instructions stated in the pattern. The sleeves are now normally added to the garment, take care to match the centre of the sleeve head to the shoulder seam. Ideally stretch the sleeve head into the armhole and stitch in place, if the sleeve head is too large for the armhole then check your tension as your knitting may be too loose. Join the underarm and side seams. Slip stitch any pockets or pocket lining into place and sew on buttons corresponding to the button holes lining up the outside edge of the button with the edging join or seam.

Carefully press your finished garment again to the measurements stated on the size diagram.

DIGITAL CHARTS
If you wish to receive a PDF version of this book then please send an email to: info@mariewallin.com with your request.

ENLARGING CHARTS
Use the PDF version of the book to enlarge the charts. If a chart is split across two or four pages, then print all sections and join together to form one large chart.

AFTERCARE
Ensure that you wash and dry your garment according to the care instructions stated on the British Breeds ball bands. Reshape your garment when slightly damp and then carefully press to size again.

BUTTONS
The buttons used in this collection were kindly supplied by **Textile Garden**, 1 Highland Croft, Steyning, BN44 3RF, UK
Telephone: +44 (0) 1903 815759 or +44 (0) 7736 904109
Email: sales@textilegarden.com · Web: www.textilegarden.com

EXPERIENCE RATING
For guidance only.
●○○ suitable for a beginner knitter with a little experience.
●●○ suitable for a knitter with average ability.
●●● suitable for the experienced knitter

BRITISH BREEDS STOCKISTS
Please refer to the stockist list on the yarn page of
www.mariewallin.com

KNITTING ABBREVIATIONS

K	knit
P	purl
st(s)	stitch(es)
inc	increas(e)(ing)
dec	decreas(e)(ing)
st st	stocking stitch (one row K, one row P)
g st	garter stitch (K every row)
beg	begin(ning)
foll	following
rem	remain(ing)
rev st st	reverse stocking stitch (one row P, one row K)
rep	repeat
alt	alternate
cont	continue
patt	pattern
tog	together
mm	millimetres
cm	centimetres
in(s)	inch(es)
RS	right side
WS	wrong side
sl	slip 1 one stitch
psso	pass slip stitch over
p2sso	pass 2 slipped stitches over
tbl	through back of loop
M1	make one stitch by picking up the horizontal loop before the next stitch and knitting into the back of it
M1P	make one stitch by picking up the horizontal loop before the next stitch and purling into the back of it
yfwd	yarn forward
yrn	yarn round needle
meas	measures
0	no stitches, times or rows
-	no stitches, times or rows for that size
yon	yarn over needle
yfrn	yarn forward round needle
wyib	with yarn at back

credits

I would like to thank the following wonderful people who have helped to make this book possible:

Moy Williams - Photography
Georgia Waters - Model
James Hearn - Model
Frances Prescott - Hair & Make Up
Sue Whiting - Pattern Writer
Tricia McKenzie - Pattern Checker
Textile Garden - Buttons
Mark Wallin - Graphic Design

A massive thank you to my team of very talented knitters: Irene Jackson, Andrea McHugh, Amanda Golland, Rowena Gillen, Mary Leeson, Juliana Yeo, Janet Taplin, Avella Reid and Gina Couch.

Photographed on location at the Langdale Estate and Shacklabank Farm, Cumbria

First published in 2022 by
Marie Wallin Designs Ltd.,
Park House, Low Abbotside, Askrigg,
Leyburn, DL8 3JH, England.
Email: info@mariewallin.com

Printed in England by Lion FPG Limited

British Library Cataloguing in Publication Data.
A catalogue record for this book is available from the British Library.

ISBN 978-1-9164008-5-6